How God Speaks To Me

Learning to Hear the Voice of God

Dr. Bettie M. Ferguson

Inspiring Voices®

A Service of **Guideposts**

Inspiring Voices books may be ordered through booksellers or by contacting:

Inspiring Voices
1663 Liberty Drive
Bloomington, IN 47403
www.inspiringvoices.com
1-(866) 697-5313

Because of the dynamic nature of the Internet, any web addresses or links contained in this book may have changed since publication and may no longer be valid. The views expressed in this work are solely those of the author and do not necessarily reflect the views of the publisher, and the publisher hereby disclaims any responsibility for them.

Any people depicted in stock imagery provided by Thinkstock are models, and such images are being used for illustrative purposes only. Certain stock imagery © Thinkstock.

Unless otherwise stated, all Scripture references are taken from the Kings James Version of the Bible.

Scripture quotations listed NLT are taken from the Holy Bible, New Living Translation, copyright © 1996, 2004, 2007 by Tyndale House Foundation. Used by permission of Tyndale House Publishers Inc., Carol Stream, Illinois 60188.

The author may have emphasized some words in Scripture quotations which are not emphasized in the original Bible versions.

ISBN: 978-1-4624-0442-1 (sc)
ISBN: 978-1-4624-0441-4 (e)

Library of Congress Control Number: 2012922425

Printed in the United States of America

Inspiring Voices rev. date: 1/18/2013

Dedication

How God Speaks To Me is dedicated first to God for inspiring me to write and tell others of His desire for intimate communion and the miracles that come from being guided by His voice!

To all who desire to experience the inner peace and joy that come from the blessing of knowing that God of the universe, maker of Heaven and earth has a deep, passionate, unending love for you. When you know Him you will hear Him.

As you read the pages of this book, let it minister to your spirit and lead you on a journey into a personal relationship with God. He will lavish on you His love, mercy, grace, peace, and protection and will accomplish miracles, signs, and wonders through your life.

Contents

Preface

How God Speaks To Me, "Learning to Hear The Voice Of God" was forged out of one woman's dramatic and sometimes traumatic experiences. In the midst of her joys and sorrows; triumphs and tragedies, the Holy Spirit of God and the Lord Jesus Christ entered her life bringing hope, encouragement, and comfort.

As you search these pages for the treasures of truth, you will find yourself on a pathway of discovery where you will begin to tap into the realm of the spirit. There you will find that the One who knows you by name and understands your deepest desires will speak to you. He loves you and has your best interest at heart. As He allures you into a place of intimacy, you will begin to hear, discern, and respond in faith to the voice of God Almighty.

Whether you are beginning your Christian journey or have matured into a fuller stature in Christ, you will be both challenged and inspired. How God Speaks To Me will compel you to greater devotion as you open your heart to its message.

My most passionate heartfelt prayer is that with this book, God will bless and enrich every life it touches. We truly are bound together in the family of God through Christ and the precious Holy Spirit.

Acknowledgments

How God Speaks To Me would not be possible without the love, encouragement, and support of my family and friends. To my daughter and prayer partner Sonya Nelson, thank you for the countless hours spent praying for our family, the church, the grandchildren, and this project. You truly are an inspiration. You comforted me through the peaks and valleys of my emotional cataclysms and encouraged me to live my dreams. Because of that, this book has become a reality.

A million thanks to my husband and best friend Charles for your love and support. You continue to be a major source of strength and encouragement to me.

Members of Faith In Action Deliverance Ministries, thank you for your love, support, encouragement, and prayers. You make doing the Father's will less challenging.

Friends and Bible Study Group at South Florida Reception Center, thank you for your prayers. Our weekly Bible studies are thought provoking and inspirational. Your encouragement and nudging compelled me to complete this venture.

Introduction

The ultimate blessing for the Body of Christ is having the ability to hear, recognize, and discern the voice of God. When we minister to hurting people, we want to know that we are not alone and that we are simply instruments God uses to accomplish His works in the earth. The questions we are confronted with are: Does God really speak to humans? Can we actually hear, and discern the voice of Almighty, Immortal God?

These and many other questions will be answered as you peruse through the pages of this book. I recommend that you take your time reading the book. Read and reread the passages that personally speak to you. Perhaps, something will spark a memory or cause you to pause and reflect on a time where you might have heard God speak, but were not sure.

When I first began hearing God speak, I was confused and confounded. I had no knowledge of God. I knew of Him, but I did not know Him and wondered why He would speak to someone as unknowledgeable as me.

I am still amazed, grateful, and inspired today, more than two decades later. I am amazed because God loves us so intensely that He longs to communicate with us. I am grateful because He chooses His people as instruments of His grace, mercy, and love. I am inspired to share the wonderful blessings that come from hearing the Almighty Immortal God speak personally to His children.

I encourage you to fine-tune your spiritual ears to hear God's voice. He is constantly speaking. He speaks to guide us and give warning of things to come. That nudging in your spirit might be God trying to get your attention.

In the beginning, I was shocked and surprised by His voice. Having no prior knowledge of His miraculous, wonder-working power, I was too embarrassed to ask questions for fear of appearing ignorant. I felt the need to shield my lack of knowledge from my fellow Christian brothers and sisters. They all seemed so spiritual. I later learned that many of my fellow parishioners did not share experiences of systematically hearing God's voice. I am grateful that I had not been too churched or filled with religiosity when God began to reveal His voice.

Let this book guide you on the pathway of discovery where you will begin to tap into the spiritual realm; a place where you will hear, discern, and respond in faith, to the voice of God.

Chapter One

Hearing The Voice Of God

*O*ver the years, as I have become more sensitive to the voices I hear speaking to me; I realize that there are several types of voices that I clearly hear. With the many voices clamoring for my attention, it became important for me to learn to distinguish each one in order to distinctly discern the voice of God.

I discovered that my own voice is the most obvious and familiar voice I hear. The voices of others; family and friends are the second most familiar voices I hear. The third type of voice I discovered was the voice of the devil. This voice was most often spoken through subjective thoughts impressed upon my mind like flaming arrows, through worldly ideas, impressions, and viewpoints. The devil is deceitful and has many crafty ways in which he speaks. I am learning to extinguish the fiery arrows of the evil one (Eph. 6:16). If what is being spoken conflicts with God's Word, then what you hear is not from God.

The fourth and final voice is the most important, but at times, it is the most subtle. It is the voice of God. God speaks to His children, but He speaks to the heart and spirit because that is where the Holy Spirit resides in us.

In the beginning, I had difficulty distinguishing the voice of God, because I was unfamiliar with the ways in which the heavenly Father communicated with His children. I had no idea that God spoke directly to His people with the exception of reading the Bible. I have since learned that hearing the voice of God is not a science, it's all about relationship.

Since I began cultivating a personal and intimate relationship with God, there are times when I can distinctly hear Him speak. His voice displays itself audibly on occasions, through dreams, and visions at other times. I also hear the voice of God while reading and meditating on the Bible, listening to the teachings of other ministers; and often, through times of personal or corporate praise and worship.

Learning to hear and discern the voice of God has been an exciting journey, it has been the ultimate blessing for my Christian journey. It is a process, where I have begun to experience God on a more personal and intimate level. I now understand that God is very much alive and desires to be an active part of our daily lives. He is interested in every minute detail of our lives.

My first experience with hearing God speak came surprisingly and unexpectedly many years ago. I was new in my Christian walk and unaware of the ways of God. I was not aware that the Lord could speak audibly to humans in modern times. In 1988, the Lord began to transform my life in such a radical and profound way that it still amazes me today. I give Him glory, honor, and praise for my transformation.

From the time I accepted Christ and began to walk with Him, He has performed one miracle after another in my life. The greatest and most precious was the gift of Salvation. This blessing has so completely changed my life; it is miraculous, marvelous, and wonderful.

Receiving Salvation was the beginning of a relationship with the Lord Jesus Christ that has transcended every area of my life and exceeded every expectation. After my new birth, the Heavenly Father began divinely guiding me through *"His still small voice and open visions."*

In the beginning, His voice and visions would occur while I was in deep prayer or during praise and worship. They appeared as, what I refer to as *"open-dreams,"* similar to out-of-body experiences. I could actually see with what was referred to in my childhood as "my spiritual eyes." These magnificent visions were the Lord's way of communicating with me through His divine wisdom. Often these visions concerned current events or some future event of my life, and I was always part of the vision, actively or as an onlooker.

When God spoke in those visions, I could hear or comprehend with my spiritual ears. Sometimes the voice was a whisper; other times, it was loud and thunderous. These visions played a very significant role in strengthening my Christian walk. Guided by Divine Wisdom and Enlightenment, I have learned to trust God totally and completely, realizing that He is divinely guiding, directing, and orchestrating my life.

In the Old Testament, God spoke to the Israelites in an audible voice, in visions, and through His prophets. When He spoke audibly, they realized they served a personal God who was Ruler over all creation, not just part of it (Deut. 4:15–20). And because they heard the voice of God, they knew they were unique among all the people of the earth (v.33).

Hearing the voice of God was a frightening experience for the Israelites. But God wanted to terrify them in order to instill a godly reverence in them that would keep them from sinning (Ex. 20:18–20; Deut. 4:36; 5:23–29). He gave the Israelites the Ten Commandments in an audible voice because keeping the commands of a Holy God would be the most important and difficult task they would ever encounter.

Likewise, when God speaks to us in an audible voice, it means we must prepare for challenges. Clarity of His voice may be the thing that gives us the power and assurance to endure any trials, temptations, or testing. If God had not begun speaking to me audibly, I might not have continued serving Him. I had no point of reference to knowing or following Him. I did not attend church or consistently read my Bible to know Him. No one I personally knew had shared with me the supernatural power of God. Hearing His voice taught me that He is real. Being led by His voice sustained me in times of sheer desperation. I can now say, I truly know God…He is real!

Chapter Two

God Speaks To Me

*W*hen God speaks to me, sometimes it's a single word; other times it is a phrase, but often, it is a complete dialogue between my Heavenly Father and me. In the beginning, I was not sure what was happening or why I was having these inspirational dialogues.

It all began in 1988 after I met an evangelist and his fiancé at the Homestead Air Force Base Exchange (BX) Mall in Homestead, Florida. The couple witnessed to me about salvation and the Lord Jesus Christ; then led me into a prayer of salvation where I made my confession of faith. Before they left the mall, the couple handed me a New Testament Pocket Bible and instructed me to begin reading and studying my Bible. They further, encouraged me to find a church that teaches the Word of God.

I thought that would be simple enough and began reading and studying my Bible daily. Finding a church that felt right took much longer since I was not accustomed to attending church anyway. I finally found a small storefront church in Perrine, Florida. It was an excellent place of worship for me. The pastor, his wife, and the people of the congregation were wonderful, God loving people. They embraced me and made me feel loved and accepted.

I didn't expect anything spectacular to occur, but I was happy to be attending church on a regular basis for the first time in my life. My past experience with church attendance was as a child. I would sometimes attend Sunday School, and once in a while stay for a regular service. That is, on the rare occasions when I attended.

I never experienced miracles, signs, and wonders operating in those churches. I had never heard of the Holy Spirit of God having personal encounters with His people. I had not seen or heard of the gifts of the Spirit, nor seen them in operation. And there was no move of the Spirit. Perhaps, I was not there often enough to hear those messages or experience the miraculous.

My life has been radically different since my encounter with that couple at the air force base mall. On the day that I made my confession of faith in the Lord Jesus Christ, I knew something had changed. It seemed as though I was seeing with new eyes. The sky had a brightness and brilliance I had never before seen. Colors were sharp, crisp, and clear. My ears became super sensitive to sound. I was truly born-again. I had become a new creature, old things had passed away, all things had become new (2 Cor. 5:17). I was exhilarated about my new life—still I had no great expectations! I had never experienced the miraculous power of God, with the exception of receiving salvation.

Since the time I accepted Jesus Christ as my Lord and Savior, my Heavenly Father has forever changed my life. He immediately began manifesting Himself through signs and wonders, performing one miracle after another.

From the very beginning, God began to speak to me and show me visions during Bible study and prayer meetings. I felt as though the Holy Spirit Himself was teaching me. Timing seemed urgent and God began to utilize me in His service almost immediately. Often, I would hear His voice during praise and worship services in church. I will share many of these experiences in a later chapter.

Today God speaks to His people primarily through dreams, visions, and His Word (the Bible). He speaks through circumstances, revelations, and the church. He also speaks through His apostles, prophets, evangelists, pastors, and teachers (Eph. 4:11). If you will spend time getting to know Him, I believe the Father will speak to you.

When God began speaking to me, I didn't know why or what to do with the revelations being unveiled. He sometimes had to speak repeatedly and loudly to get my attention. For example, one morning years ago, I was in a hurry to get to work on time, but was hungry and began searching for something to prepare for lunch. I distinctly heard the Lord softly speak, the word "*Fast*." Who's speaking? I wondered. I was home alone, but heard the word '*fast*' as though someone was standing next to me.

I could not find anything to prepare quickly; since I was running late for work, I abruptly abandoned the idea of bagging a lunch. I decided to stop at a Burger King near my job and pick up breakfast instead. While standing in the line at Burger King, I again heard the voice of the Lord say, "FAST." I asked myself, "Why am I hearing this?" I had no idea that the Lord was trying to get my attention. How could I know? This was all new to me. I was absolutely clueless to the fact that the Almighty Immortal God could speak to mere mortals in this manner, especially me.

The line at Burger King was barely moving, so I abandoned the idea of waiting any longer and left, deciding to wait until I reached the job to find something more appealing. At the time, I worked as an independent vendor at the Homestead Air Force Base Exchange Mall.

I arrived at work and strolled into the Baskin & Robbins Ice Cream Shop, knowing I could find something appetizing to curb my hunger. As I stood reading the menu, I again heard more loudly this time, "FAST!" There was no mistake—the Lord was speaking to re-emphasize my need to fast. I was clueless about fasting and didn't know why someone would fast. I was new in my Christian experience and had only recently begun attending church.

In my ignorance to the things of God, I mentioned to the elderly store clerk in the ice cream shop that I kept hearing the word, "fast." To my surprise, this woman began to rebuke me rather harshly. "Don't eat or drink anything; how dare you quench the Holy Spirit of God" (1 Thess. 5:17), she scolded! Now thoroughly confused, I quickly left that ice cream shop, abandoning the idea of eating or drinking. I was unfamiliar with fasting, and knew nothing of the operations of the Holy Spirit of God. Not knowing what to do, I prayed for wisdom and guidance. The Lord impressed upon my spirit that I should fast for three days. I immediately asked myself, "How am I going to fast for three days?" I had never gone one day without eating and rarely missed a meal. However, I resisted the urge to eat or drink for the next three days.

Not knowing what to expect, I was a bit nervous since this was my first fast; but I prayed and meditated on the Word of God throughout those three days. Surprisingly, the Lord sustained me and I was able to get through those days with ease—by the grace, mercy, and love of God. Through it all, I quickly learned that obedience is better than sacrifice according to Scripture. "And Samuel said, hath the Lord as great delight in burnt offerings and sacrifices as in obeying the voice of the Lord? Behold, to obey is better than sacrifice and to hearken than the fat of rams" (1 Sam. 15:22). The New Living Translation states the verse this way: "What is more pleasing to the Lord: your burnt offerings and sacrifices or your obedience to His voice? Obedience is better than sacrifice, and submission is better than offering the fat of rams."

Several days after I ended my fast, I experienced the strong, powerful hand of Almighty God and His divine protection. It was on a Wednesday night in the summer of 1988. I had attended a church meeting and left my thirteen year old daughter and nine year old niece home watching a movie. During the meeting, I heard the telephone ring in the church office and instinctively knew, by divine revelation that the call was for me. The secretary answered the telephone and promptly came to tell me I needed to rush home, there was an emergency.

I hastened home, praying all the way; to find that my home had been burglarized with the children inside. The burglar had entered my home by removing slats from the jalousie style windows in a back bedroom of the house. The children said they heard a noise but before they could get to the back bedroom, the young man was kicking open the locked door of my son's bedroom. The girls only had enough time to hide inside a small closet in my daughter's bedroom. The girls had only enough time to hide in a small closet in my daughter's bedroom.

The burglar ransacked my home, stealing money, jewelry, electronics; taking video games, my son's class ring, and small household items. He entered my daughter's bedroom, rummaged through her things, never realizing the girls were hiding inside the closet only inches from where he stood. That is what I call the divine protection of Almighty God! He placed His shield of protection over my children and kept them safe from harm and danger.

A similar story is found in the Book of Esther Chapter Four. Plans were being made to annihilate an entire community of Jewish people. The only hope for saving her people from death and destruction was for Esther, the queen to speak up. If she remained silent, it would mean certain death for her and all her people. "Then Esther sent this reply to her Uncle Mordecai: Go and gather all the Jews of Susa and fast for me. Do not eat or drink for three days, night or day. My maids and I will do the same. And then, though it is against the law, I will go in to see the king. If I must die, I must die" (Esther 4:14–16). Esther called a three day fast that saved the Jewish people throughout an entire empire. God called me on a three day fast that shielded, protected, and possibly saved the lives of my children.

The Holy Spirit insisted on me fasting and spoke repeatedly to get my attention. Perhaps, He was teaching me to hear and recognize His voice, or maybe; He was teaching me obedience. I don't know, but I thank God that I never had to wonder what would have happened had I not heeded His voice and fasted. I am grateful for Him leading me to the lady in the ice cream shop, without her wisdom, I would not have known the steps to take. God always leads, guides, directs, and protects.

During that time, I realized that our Heavenly Father is the ultimate expression of love. He loves us intensely. We are made in His likeness and image and are the objects of His affection. He loves us with a love that is perfect, unconditional, and perpetual. We are the highest form of His creation, having the ability to perceive, receive, and reciprocate His love. God revealed this magnificent truth to me when He led me on that fast and divinely protected my family.

As I stated, I did not understand the things of God and He had to speak several times before I knew I needed to respond. In the Book of First Samuel Chapter Three, when Samuel was a young boy serving in the house of the Lord with the prophet Eli, God began to speak to him. Scripture tells us that God called Samuel three times before he realized that the Lord was trying to reveal a message. Like Samuel, I did know the Lord, and His Words *'voice'* had not yet been revealed to me (1 Sam. 3:7).

As was the case with Samuel, when God first called him, He went to Eli, thinking Eli was calling. The prophet Eli instructed Samuel how to respond after the third time God called. The Holy Spirit led me to the lady in the ice cream shop so that I would know how to respond to His voice. It is extremely difficult to follow God's instructions, if we don't know when He is speaking.

It is not uncommon for people who are young in their Christian walk to be of the misconception that God only speaks to those who hold high leadership positions in the church. This is not the case. It was not the case with Eli and Samuel. Eli was the priest and held the proper position and status as a representative of God in the Tabernacle; but God did not speak to Eli, He spoke to the boy, Samuel (1 Sam. 3:1–14). When God Began speaking to me, I had no biblical knowledge, status, or prestige.

God speaks to those who are open and receptive to His Spirit. If we seek Him, we will find Him. If we seek Him, He will show us how to walk with Him. If we seek Him, He will speak to us, and we will hear from Him. He will never fail to provide divine guidance, protection, peace, and comfort.

God says, "And ye shall seek Me and find Me, when you shall search for Me with all your heart" (Jer. 29:13). He's waiting for us!

This was the first of many divine revelations from my Heavenly Father.

Most gracious Heavenly Father, I thank You for being our Jehovah-Nissi, (the Lord our Banner); and thanks for shielding, protecting, and keeping us safe from danger (Ex. 17:15). Amen!

Chapter Three

Ways God Speaks

Throughout the Bible, from Genesis to Revelation, God has spoken to His people, and we can anticipate Him speaking to us. He spoke to Adam and Eve in the Garden of Eden. He spoke to Abraham. He spoke to Noah, the judges, kings, and the prophets. God spoke to the disciples through His Son, Jesus Christ. God spoke to the early church, He spoke to Saul on the Road to Damascus and He spoke to John on the Isle of Patmos.

In the Bible, God spoke repeatedly and in various ways. In the Old and New Testaments we will find Him speaking through:

- Face to Face encounters (Genesis Chapters 1–4)
- Visions (Genesis Chapter 15)
- Angels (Genesis 16)
- Dreams (Genesis 28:10–19)
- Burning Bush (Exodus 3:2–4)
- Audible Voice (Exodus 4–40)

- During the Age of the Law–Through His Prophets and Priests
- Still Small Voice (1 Kings 19:12)
- Prophets (2 Kings 17:13)
- Symbolic Actions (Jeremiah 18:1–12)
- During the Incarnation—He became flesh and dwelt among us (John 1:1–14)
- In the early church—By the manifestation of His Holy Spirit (Acts 2:1–4; 4:31; 10:44)
- Presently God speaks primarily through His completed revelation, the written Word of God (2 Tim. 3:16–17)

These are only a few examples of how God has chosen to speak to His people down through the ages. We must study the Scriptures to determine how to recognize the voice of our Heavenly Father, as He calls us to follow Him and guides us into divine purpose.

When God spoke, it was usually unique to that individual. Moses' burning bush experience was one such encounter (Ex. 3:2–4). No one else had encountered God speaking in like manner. Likewise, God wishes for each of us to have our own personal encounters with Him.

God speaks to His people through His Holy Spirit. He also speaks through the Bible, prayer, circumstances, and the church. He may speak any way He chooses, but when He does, He reveals Himself, His plans, and His purposes.

When God speaks, He is revealing truth. His desire is that we know, understand, and comprehend His message. The Holy Spirit is our Helper and He will help us to properly discern the Word of Truth, God's Truth. "For He, (the Holy Spirit) alone knows the mind of God" (1 Cor. 2:10–11).

When God speaks in the New Testament, we are actually engaged in a personal encounter with Him through His Son. The Gospel of John begins, "In the beginning was the Word; and the Word was with God, and the Word was God; and the Word became flesh and dwelt among us" (John 1:1, 14). The Word became flesh in the person of the Lord Jesus Christ.

Throughout the Gospels, we see Jesus in the flesh calling His disciples, teaching them, exhorting them, equipping them for service; performing miracles with them, even serving them. Today He is calling us; you and me into service. We serve Him by serving others.

Jesus exhorted, healed, and delivered the people so that they could enjoy a more intimate relationship with His Father. Likewise, the Holy Spirit is calling us so that we may lead others to Jesus Christ, the only begotten Son of God. We are empowered by the Holy Spirit, our Helper to get the job done! One point to remember is that one must know and understand how God speaks and when He is speaking. To know and discern how God speaks requires that we spend time basking in His presence.

We must study the Bible and spend time meditating on His Word to see how He uses His Word to make confirmation in our spirits. Jesus exhorted His disciples to watch as well as pray (Matt. 26:41). We must also watch and see what God is doing in our circumstances. He may speak through the events of our lives. He has spoken to me in the church, in the home, on the job, in the car, and various other places. He may speak to you any place—at anytime.

I have learned that God is awesome, amazing, and Omniscient, all-wise. Once He spoke the word "JEZEBEL" in a church service, during high praise and worship. This word of knowledge was concerning a young lady, who was dating my son. Jezebel is not a modern day term, so I knew the Holy Spirit was revealing the spiritual truth of a stronghold in the young lady's life; she had come to visit the church we were attending.

I was shocked, surprised, and utterly dismayed that such a lovely young woman would possess such a hideous spirit. I almost felt that it was an invasion of her privacy for me to have this knowledge. What was I to do with such revelation? Obviously, the Lord needed me to know that the young lady was being controlled by the spirit of Jezebel. I could not openly confront this young woman about the situation; it would have been too embarrassing for both of us.

Being young in my Christian walk, I did research to find out who this Jezebel character was. I discovered that Jezebel was a wicked queen, wife of the passive king, Ahab. She was a false prophetess who worshipped the false god, Baal. The Jezebel spirit is a spirit of witchcraft and rebellion. It is a controlling spirit that works through the lust of the flesh and is a powerful enemy of the body of Christ.

I am sure the young woman was not a Christian at the time, but I prayed, interceding for her salvation and deliverance. My son had recently begun trying to procure his own spiritual stability, and this relationship was a serious deterrent to his life and spiritual pursuit.

Both these young people needed help! By the grace of God, with much prayer, counseling, serious commitment, and strong determination, they managed to dedicate their lives to Christ and remained friends until shortly before my son's untimely death. Through their interactions, I was able to understand much about the Spirit of Jezebel.

Read the full story of Jezebel in (1 Kings 16:31–2 Kings 9:37). Her name is used as a synonym of evil in (Rev. 2:20–22).

Chapter Four

When God Speaks

From the various stories I share in this book, it is clear that God has numerous ways in which He speaks. He will get our attention, but sometimes it's difficult to discern His voice, or comprehend the mysterious ways in which He communicates.

The stories herein represent true accounts of sundry times that God has spoken to me. I have listed them chronologically under each heading. There have been many visions and I have heard the voice of God on numerous occasions since I began diligently serving Him.

Many times His voice or visions are instructions pertaining to my life, the lives of family members; directions for my ministry, or decisions I need to make involving my career. I have been given revelations concerning other spiritual leaders in my community. I have also been prompted to pray for the United States and other nations. When God gives spiritual insights, they are usually revealed to provide specific instructions on the direction, in which I am to intercede.

When God speaks He is revealing Himself for the good of humanity. What He reveals might be for the present or future. When He speaks, we must begin making the necessary adjustments in preparation for what He is planning to accomplish. When God speaks, the things in His mind and heart shall surely come to pass. His purpose in the earth shall be fulfilled and His Word shall stand eternally.

God speaks through dreams, visions, His Word, circumstances, revelations, church, and through His prophets. On occasion, He has spoken to me through all of the above. We may encounter Him while in deep prayer, meditation, or during praise and worship.

God has not changed; He is the same yesterday, today, and forever (Hebrew 13:8). The same way God used the prophets of the Old Testament to speak to His people, He speaks to His people today. The difference today is that we have the aid of the Holy Spirit. Again, we must become God-centered and have a personal relationship with Him, to hear Him. There is no magic formula for knowing God's voice. There is no method to follow. We hear His voice because we have relationship with Him.

I have experienced God's voice and visions by starting a simple prayer of adoration and gratitude. The prayer leads to praise, praise leads to worship; and worship catapults me into a place where the Father relishes His love on me and relinquish a multiplicity of blessings! I also receive the honor of His presence when I pray in the spirit and worship in my heavenly language (tongues).

Take time to know the Father. Pray and earnestly ask the Holy Spirit to reveal Himself. The way He speaks to you might be unique and personal. It is not one size fits all! It takes faith, patience, and practice to systematically hear God speak.

God communicates with each of us. We communicate with God by being in close relationship with Him. This relationship cannot be circumvented, if our desire is to be guided by His voice.

We sometimes go to spiritual leaders, relatives, or friends seeking advice on what we believe God is saying but God wants us to depend on Him alone. This dependency can only come through having the proper relationship with Him.

In the beginning, I made the mistake of running to people for interpretation of the visions God was revealing. I quickly discovered that God does not communicate with everyone in the same manner. Most people with whom I spoke, including some pastors had never experienced God speaking in open visions. I quickly realized that His relationship with me was unique and very personal. We must set aside time to wait and listen for God's voice. In His presence is fullness of Joy; at His right hand are pleasures for evermore (Ps. 16:11). It is when we are quiet that we most clearly hear Him.

The Prophet Elijah learned to hear the voice of God when God instructed him to stand before Him on the mountain; and the Lord passed by, and a great and mighty wind began to blow and broke the rocks into pieces. But the Lord's voice was not in the wind; after the wind, an earthquake shook the mountain, but the Lord was not speaking through the earthquake. Next, a fire began to blaze, but God's voice was not in the fire. Finally, Elijah heard God speaking in a still small voice (1 Kings 19:11-12).

Elijah realized that God does not always reveal Himself in powerful, miraculous ways. He knew the sound of the gentle whisper was God's voice. If we look for God only in large highly visible experiences; we might miss Him because He is often found gently whispering in the quietness of a humble heart. To hear His voice, we must step back from the noise and commotions of life; wait—listen humbly and quietly for His voice. In the event of an emergency or crisis, He may speak through noise and clutter.

Chapter Five

Developing Intimacy

*T*hrough life's journey, we will hear and experience the expressed love of God as we learn to fellowship with Him. When He speaks, and *He will speak*, we must promptly capture what He reveals and respond immediately.

When I became aware of the Father's love for me and His desire for intimacy with His children, I became thirsty for more of Him. I was at a point of sheer desperation and utter despair; there was no place for me to turn. Totally surrendered, I turned to God. My life was in shambles and I had finally found unconditional love and acceptance in none other than my Lord and Savior.

During the time, I discovered the Father's everlasting, undying love, and the sacrifice of His only begotten Son, for me. I fell in love with my Creator and He honored my desire for intimacy. Through this communion, I gained the privilege of being divinely guided by Love.

Knowing that my Heavenly Father loved me so unconditionally was monumental in inspiring my wanting to know Him more intimately. I was a sold out, surrendered, desperate soul with nothing to lose! I honored my heavenly Father and He honored me with His voice and His presence. I had done nothing to warrant Him loving me so deeply. I simply appreciated the Lord for His loving kindness toward me.

God's Word says, "I love those who love me, and those who seek me early shall find me" (Pro. 8:17). The Bible clearly states, if we draw nigh to God, He will draw nigh to us" (Jas. 4:8). Come near to God, my beloved, He wants to shower you with His love.

When we spend time cultivating a love relationship with God, we will have no trouble hearing and discerning His voice. Intimacy allows us to know how the Father communicates personally with each of us. There are no short cuts. Our personal experiences in hearing God speak come from spending time with Him; spending time in His Word, in prayer, and meditation. Relationship with the Father requires faith, but it also requires action.

Developing an intimate relationship with God the Father is pivotal to knowing Him and hearing Him. We should desire intimacy because our Heavenly Father wants to provide us with the full measure of His love, His majesty, His holiness, His power, His grace, and His joy. When we develop intimacy, we will begin to comprehend these powerful truths and our lives will become more enriched, empowered, and energized.

The Father loves His children and He longs to have intimate communion with us. He wants us to hear His voice and know His will. God's desire is to give us the full measure of His blessings; physically, spiritually, emotionally, and financially. The Bible declares that, "Eye hath not seen, neither ear heard, neither hath entered into the heart of man, the things which God hath prepared for them that love Him. But

God hath revealed them unto us by His Spirit: For the Spirit searches all things; yea, the deep things of God" (1 Cor. 2:9–10).

Simply put, we cannot discern, comprehend, nor understand the full measure of blessings the Father has in store for those that love Him. His desire is to do exceedingly, abundantly, above all that we can ask or think (Eph. 3:20). He reveals these powerful truths to us by His precious Holy Spirit. The Holy Spirit of God knows all things, even the heart of God and what we have received is not by the world's standard, but by the Spirit of God, so that we might know the gifts that are freely given us by our Heavenly Father (1 Cor. 2:11–12). Paraphrased.

Chapter Six

Blessings in Obedience

*I*f God speaks and we fail to obey, there may be major consequences. Case in point: In the summer of 1989, my family was traveling convoy from Miami, Florida to Plantersville, Alabama to visit with relatives. We were driving northbound on the Florida Turnpike at speeds of sixty-five to seventy-five miles per hour. I was directly behind my sister's car when I heard the voice of the Lord say, "Pray!" With all the excitement and joy of the children's voices; and the radio blaring in the background, there was no mistaking the voice of God. I recognized His *still small voice* over the noise. He did not have to shout nor repeat Himself and I did not need consultation for what to pray.

I had learned from previous experience that I needed to respond expediently when He speaks and time is of essence. When God speaks it may be a matter of life and death! I turned down the volume on the radio and proceeded to pray for the safety and protection of my family.

My prayer of protection was not only for those of us who were traveling, but for our loved ones we were leaving behind in Miami. I prayed for those we were visiting and I prayed for fellow travelers.

A frightening event took place within a few minutes of my prayer. My children and I watched in horror as my sister's car careened out-of-control right before our eyes. She took her eyes off the road for a split-second and looked toward the passenger seat to speak to her son. As she did, her car swerved into the right lane. She quickly pulled it back into the left lane but the car began to fishtail out-of-control. It suddenly began spinning in circles in the median before speeding across all southbound lanes of traffic and down a steep embankment.

It was a miracle that no other vehicle collided with my sister's vehicle. It all happened in a split-second! We could not see my sister's vehicle down the embankment. I could not tell if the car had overturned or if anyone was hurt.

Panic stricken and totally astounded by what had transpired; I quickly pulled my car safely into the median and made my way out of the vehicle. I ran across all southbound lanes of traffic frantically waving as cars, trucks, and eighteen wheelers came barreling toward me. Obviously, they had witnessed the out of control vehicle. Several truckers pulled over to assist us.

I ran down the embankment to reach the vehicle, as my sister sat panic-stricken, with both hands frozen to the steering wheel. Neither of us could speak. We simply, stared at each other in utter amazement. I asked my sister if they were okay, as she sat there, literally in shock. She stated that she and the kids were fine. The children were wide-eyed and terrified, but safe.

My sister's car had traveled down the embankment and made a u-turn as it headed back up the embankment. Instead continuing up that embankment and into traffic, the car miraculously came to an abrupt stop. I believe an angel of the Lord stopped that car in its tracks. Amazingly, no one was hurt.

With the assistance of the truckers, we guided my sister's car up the embankment, across the median, back into the northbound lanes; and continued on our journey. There was not a scratch, den, bump, or bruise. It was only by the grace of God, and my obedience to His voice that we avoided a catastrophe on the Florida Turnpike that day.

Later, when we reached our destination, I asked my sister what had happened. Her words did not surprise me. She said, "I lost total control of that vehicle. There was nothing I could do. It was *as if* a huge hand reached in and took control of the steering wheel and guided that car."

My sister was not an inexperienced driver. She drove large trucks at her job and she possessed her Commercial Driver's License (CDL) at the time. I don't have to wonder, *"what if"* I had not heeded the voice of Almighty God that day.

Thank You, Heavenly Father for Your never-ending love, mercy, grace, and powerful shield of protection.

Chapter Seven

God Speaks Through Visions

*W*e have the capacity to hear and understand God, but we must learn to listen to Him. When we listen to Him, we will hear His voice and understand His wisdom. If we follow His direction and obey His instructions, we will live an abundant and prosperous life. When God reveals Himself and His Truth to us, we must act. We will then experience the power of Truth in action. Jesus said, "And you shall know the truth and the truth shall make you free" (John 8:32). It is His truth that makes us free.

If we follow the truth, we can be free to live and love; free to give and receive, free from doubt and fear. The moment God speaks is His timing. However, His will and purpose may not be accomplished for a time in the future, as with Abraham, Noah, Moses, David, Paul, and others.

The plans and purposes of the believer must be in line with God's plans and purposes if we desire to experience the awesome power of God accomplishing greatness through our lives. Without the aid of the Spirit of God we cannot understand God's truths.

Our spirits long to hear God but there are many other things competing for our time. Families, jobs, careers, recreational activities, and ministry all seek our attention. Therefore, we must be steadfast and diligent in setting aside undivided time to hear from the Father. And we must also learn to wait and listen for His instructions. We cannot know when, where, or how to accomplish His purpose until He reveals it to us. He will reveal Himself to those who take time to develop a personal relationship with Him.

Anyone who wants to hear God's voice on a regular basis will have to become intimately acquainted with His written Word and spend time in meditation and reverence, undistracted by the cares of this world. God speaks to guide us, save us from disaster, and help us minister to others. God has also used His Word to reprove and rebuke me of my erroneous behavior.

The Bible says, All Scripture is given by inspiration of God, and is profitable for doctrine, for reproof, for correction, for instruction in righteousness (2 Tim. 3:16).

His purposes accomplished His way, always bring Him glory. Remember, "God's thoughts are not our thoughts, nor are His ways our ways" (Is. 55:8). I have received visions and heard God speak on many occasions. These occasions always bring divine revelation and instructions from the Holy Spirit. However, most occur when I'm in deep prayer or during praise and worship.

Documented in these pages are but a few visions and dialogues I've had with my Heavenly Father, but I believe they will be instrumental in helping you develop and cultivate an intimate relationship with God where you will begin to hear, discern, and respond to the voice of God.

Mission Impossible

In 1990 God spoke to me in an *open vision* during praise and worship at a Wednesday night prayer meeting. The words He spoke left me shocked and bewildered! This was my first encounter with God on such a deeply personal level. I had heard His voice and learned to recognize when He was speaking; however, I had never experienced an encounter with Him in an open vision.

The Father's concern at the time was for the condition of our nation's youth. In the vision, I saw young people; teens and young adults of all races and cultures; from all walks of life; sitting in a large arena. I heard the voice of the Lord speak the words, "Teen Christian Center." My question to God was, "Why?" He responded, "Our youth are lost, they don't know the Lord; they are caught up on drugs, sex, and violence." Needless to say, I was quite surprised to be having this dialogue.

My spirit was prepared through worship but my natural mind began to reason. Scripture tells us that the natural mind cannot comprehend the things of the Spirit, "But the natural man does not receive the things of the Spirit of God, for they are foolishness unto him; nor can he know them, because they are spiritually discerned" (1 Cor. 2:14).

I remember responding, "This is an enormous project; something of this magnitude will cost lots of money." At the time, I was struggling financially and was clueless how I would accomplish such an astronomical project. God replied, "Government grants, people will give donations." Paralyzed by fear, I responded in doubt, "I don't know enough, I'm not ready." I allowed doubt and fear to overcome me and instantaneously all communication ceased.

Coming out of the vision, I discovered that I was still standing in the church with people who were praying and wondered what had just happened. God had catapulted me into a realm of the spirit I did not previously know existed, and had no idea was possible. Could God really use me in such an awesome and profound way?

Having little knowledge of the immensity and power of God, I allowed the spirit of fear to rob me of the blessings He had for me, the youth of this nation—perhaps, the world. This was obviously, a God-sized project, and I missed the opportunity to effect change on a God-sized level because of fear.

I have since learned that when God speaks, He has a purpose in mind. When God speaks, He is ready to accomplish something colossal. When God spoke to Abram in Genesis Chapter Twelve, He was preparing to build a nation. God spoke to Abram when He did because it was then, that He was ready to begin building. Abram responded, by making the necessary adjustments in his life and immediately obeyed God's instructions. Timing is everything!

The moment God speaks is the moment we must respond. We must not assume that we have the next few weeks, months, or years to think about it. We believers must be in constant communion, with Him daily. He is the very source of our lives, our strength, hope, peace, and joy. He's our Savior and Lord, our Comforter, and Mediator. He desires to be our total source. When God gives the Word, we must continue in the direction He's leading until that which He purposes comes to pass.

When we learn to recognize His voice, we will begin to know His will. When God purposes a thing, He reveals His thoughts to us. He may do this in many ways; through our hearts and minds, through words, His voice, or pictures. He may use books, the Bible, scenes from a movie, scenes from nature, dreams, visions, and His spoken Word. He may communicate any way He chooses, using any medium of transmission He chooses. He may use any person, any place, and He may speak at any time, but we must be attuned to hear and respond.

Through this experience, I learned that God needs someone with a willingness of heart, and a spirit of obedience to walk by faith when He speaks. I'm sure Abram did not know where he was going when the Lord spoke to him and said, "Leave your country, your people, and your father's household and go to the land I will show you. I will make you into a great nation and I will bless you; I will make your name great, and 'you will be a blessing.' I will bless those who bless you, and curse those who curse you; and all peoples on earth will be blessed through you" (Gen. 12:1-3). The thing Abraham had was faith and confidence in the One who had spoken. Unlike Abram, I failed to act when God spoke, but He did not stop speaking. Although, He has never again spoken to me about that project, He still speaks to me today.

Let us remember the words of Paul to Timothy, "God has not given us the spirit of fear; but of power, of love, and of a sound mind" (2 Tim. 1:7).

Demon of Destruction

One night while in Bible Study during the praise and worship service, I was caught up in another open vision. God revealed to me that there was an unfamiliar spirit in my home. The year was 1989. In the vision, I saw myself standing in the living room of my home. Initially, I only observed the setting and furnishing. At the time, I had no interest in praying about my furniture. All the amazing things the Lord could accomplish through my life, why furniture? I wondered. But as I continued looking around, right before my eyes appeared an unfamiliar spirit. It was standing there looking at me.

Talk about shocked and surprised! This situation was frightening, but oh, so humbling. Certainly I had not forgotten the amazing Omniscient, Omnipresent power of Almighty God. Actually, I had never really learned this amazing aspect.

Nonetheless, this was a single square shaped entity about three feet tall and two feet wide. It was a deep maroon or burgundy in color. Although it was a single entity, my spirit sensed that it was three-in-one. I knew that it did not belong there, and wondered; what is this? Where did it come from? How long has it been here? A thousand other questions ran through my mind.

As I continued looking at that unfamiliar spirit, I glimpsed something white from the left side of my face. I turned, and there was the most beautiful, white cloud I had ever seen, hovering near the ceiling. The cloud was thick, heavy, and whiter than snow. The beauty of the cloud caused a feeling of peace to envelop me. The cloud hovered for a few seconds, before ascending toward the heavens.

I have no precedence or explanation for the unfamiliar spirit or cloud. I believe the cloud represented the glory and protection of the Lord, until I was able to take authority over the situation.

Scriptures provide powerful references to the glory of God appearing in a cloud. Exodus 16:10 offers this wonderful example: "And it came to pass, as Aaron spoke unto the whole congregation of the Children of Israel, that they looked toward the wilderness, and behold, the glory of the Lord appeared in the cloud."

Exodus19:9 says, "And the Lord said unto Moses, lo, I come unto thee in a thick cloud, that the people may hear when I speak with thee and believe thee forever."

Meanwhile, empowered by His glory, I turned back and looked at that unfamiliar spirit, still standing there, and commanded it to

"GET OUT IN THE NAME OF JESUS!" The demon left, walking down the sidewalk.

Prior to the vision, my home was in utter disarray. There were plumbing problems, electrical problems, the roof was leaking, along with a host of other infrastructure issues. The moment one repair was completed there was another to be done. The children were at odds with each other and my contentious marriage had recently ended.

The Holy Spirit revealed that the unfamiliar spirit was a demon of destruction. When I took authority in the Name of Jesus and cast out that demon of destruction, chaos and confusion left along with it. I still had to complete the repairs on my home, but there now were peace and contentment, where there had been confusion and discord.

I now realize that God is real, but demons are also real. We are conditioned to interact in the natural realm to things we can taste, touch, hear, smell, and see. I am not sure why God has chosen to reveal these spiritual revelations to me, but I am grateful. He has made me a prayer warrior so that I can join Him in spiritual warfare here on earth, NOW!

I thank You El-Shaddai, Almighty God (Gen. 17:1) for your omnipresent (Ps. 139:7–10) and for being our mighty shield of protection.

Help Holy Spirit!

On another occasion in 1991, I had a similar experience. The venue was the same. It occurred at church during the praise and worship service. I saw myself standing in the dining room of a relative's home. In the vision, my relative appeared to be very angry, upset, and distraught. I sensed that these emotions were directed toward me and asked myself, "How can this be? Where is this anger coming from?"

I dearly love my relative and was unaware to any ill-will or animosity between us. I continued praying in the spirit. Time was of no essence. I discovered that time simply does exist in the spiritual realm. The scenes of this event played out as on a movie screen, with me watching the events unfold. My relative appeared livid. I could see the rage in her face, and I could see her mouth spewing contempt, but I did not hear the words.

I dug deep, interceding for her. I needed the almighty power of El-Shaddai. I continued praying, asking God for her deliverance. In the next scene, I saw my relative sitting at her dining room table. Thinking that the victory had been won, I prepared to move to the next thing on the Holy Spirit's agenda. But there again, was my relative furious and belligerent.

The Holy Spirit revealed to me that this was a '*stronghold of anger.*' This knowledge was nothing I could have known. In the natural, everything about our relationship appeared normal. Only the Spirit of Truth Himself could cause me comprehend the things being revealed. The Holy Spirit is the Revealer of hidden things of the heart. Scripture confirms that, "The Lord will both bring to light the hidden things of darkness and reveal the counsels of the heart" (1 Cor. 4:5).

I continued interceding; desperately pleading for the Holy Spirit to heal my relative's wounded spirit. I decided that I would not end my prayer or leave the church until that spirit of anger had been overcome. I'm not sure how long I was caught up in the vision, but I continued praying until at last, I saw my relative sitting on her bed with her hands folded on her lap. Her head was bowed and she appeared calm.

Coming out of the vision, the strangest phenomenon occurred. I experienced every emotion a human can experience, in a split-second. I felt joy and pain; happiness and sadness; I wanted to laugh and cry; I wanted to run and shout. All these emotions encompassed me instantly and simultaneously.

I was spiritually and emotionally devastated, knowing that someone I love so deeply had these malicious thoughts concerning me. How do I handle this crisis? I prayed, asking the Lord for guidance. The Lord responded, "Continue to pray for her and show her love." I did that, but I also spoke to this relative who denied any problems. But I knew the truth. Jesus said, "And ye shall know the truth and the truth shall make you free" (John 8:32). The hidden things of the heart had been revealed. My relative and I have been estranged for more than two decades, and I have made countless attempts to try and find resolve, to no avail. But even now, I continue to pray for her complete and total deliverance.

Interestingly, when caught up in the spirit, my surroundings—the people, buildings, sanctuary, all fade into nothingness. The only things visible are the Holy Spirit's revelations on the screen of my mind. However, during these inspirational encounters, my physical senses are intact; I can think, reason, and make decisions. I don't know how He does this, but let me reaffirm—God is awesome, all encompassing, and totally amazing!

Most gracious Heavenly Father, I pray for my family's salvation, healing, and deliverance. Perform a miracle today, amen!

Surviving The Storm

In August of 1992, the Holy Spirit spoke to me while I was home cleaning. He simply said, "PRAY!" I had learned to hear and obey His voice. Therefore, when He spoke, I promptly entered my bedroom and lay upon my bed and began to worship in the spirit. The Holy Spirit began a dialogue with me saying, "The hurricane is going to hit Miami."

I was startled and fearful, but the Holy Spirit spoke again and said, "Don't worry you will be safe, 'pray' for the people of Miami." I am very grateful that the Holy Spirit did not permit me to see the coming devastation and destruction in that vision.

I continued worshipping in the spirit and thanked my Heavenly Father in advance for His protection of my family and the people of Miami. Coming out of the vision, I only knew to trust Him. I had been given divine revelation knowledge.

I had never experienced the destruction of a hurricane but I trusted that the Lord would protect us, as He promised. I have learned that His promises are sure and steadfast.

About a week after the dialogue, it was broadcasted on all the local news stations that the southernmost part of Miami, where we lived, would take a direct hit from Hurricane Andrew. This was the first hurricane of the season and it was estimated to be a category five, packing winds up to one hundred seventy-five miles per hour.

Hurricane Andrew did hit Miami on August 24, 1992. The destruction was catastrophic. Homes were destroyed, thousands of families were displaced. It cost billions in property damage. It was reported that fifteen people died as a direct result of Hurricane Andrew; which was tragic but also miraculous, considering the depth of destruction. Hurricane Andrew was also reported as the costliest hurricane in the history of the United States, at that time.

Before the storm, I contacted my family and some of my friends assuring them that we had space in our home, if anyone needed shelter. No one expected the storm to be as calamitous as it was; so everyone buckled down in their own homes or found public shelters.

During the hurricane, the Holy Spirit divinely guided and protected my family. We had no storm shutters, or protective covering on the doors or windows but, God gave specific instructions during the dark of night on making it safely through the storm.

When the wind began to roar and the window panes started shattering; a powerful wind force entered our home sounding like a freight train roaring through. It made three turns; a left through the living-room; a right turn through the kitchen; and a left turn to miraculously exit the backdoor. I believe an angel of the Lord guided that wind force through our home and by God's grace, it never touched anything inside.

We later discovered that Hurricane Andrew was accompanied by tornados. I'm not sure, if it was the hurricane, or a tornado that contributed to the thunderous noise inside our home, but El-Shaddai protected us.

After the wind force passed through, the Holy Spirit spoke again and said, "Save the back door!" My fifteen year old daughter and I fought with all our strength to save the door. We would pull the door in, and the wind would pull it out again; but we held on, refusing to let go. We knew we were in a tug of war with the forces of nature. We struggled with that door for ten to fifteen minutes, until a powerful force of wind miraculously blew from the outside and sealed the door shut. That was the mighty hand of God safeguarding us as He had promised!

My husband was busy in the front of the house trying to find something—anything to shield the front windows. I remember him commenting, "It's going to be embarrassing in the morning; we had advance warning and were not prepared." He did not have to worry about being embarrassed because boards and shutters were no match for the powerful force of Hurricane Andrew.

As the sliver of dawn began to peek through the darkness of night and we could see outside, the devastation and destruction were indescribably shocking. Houses crumbled. Roofs were blown away, tossed like Frisbees. Doors and windows were found blocks away. Homes that were surrounded by boards and shutters now had furniture and personal property blown through huge gaping holes in walls and roofs. Cars, trucks, tractor trailers were overturned, flipped and flung like toys.

Entire trailer parks were completely obliterated. Hugh trees were uprooted. Telephone and electric poles snapped like twigs. Hurricane Andrew left behind tons of rubble and mountains of debris! There were no electricity, water, or telephone service for weeks, months in many cases. It was critical. Thousands of people were left without food, water, shelter, or security. It was physically and emotionally devastating. It took years for families to find some sense of normalcy, many never did—they simply packed up and left town.

My family along with many of Miami's residents sustained very little property damage and no bodily injury from Hurricane Andrew. However, the psychological effects penetrated deeply. It's difficult to witness such pain and suffering, and not be greatly impacted. This was a time when families, neighbors, communities, even strangers came together to rebuild that which had been tragically lost.

As painful and devastating as it was; God kept us safe as He had promised. He has spoken to me on numerous occasions the words, "I am your Keeper" (Ps. 121:5). The Father has not promised a life free from danger, but He promises to be a very-present help in our times of trouble (Ps. 46:1).

When we face imminent danger, the psalmist provides the assurance of God's powerful shield of protection declaring, "He who dwells in the secret place of the Most High shall abide under the shadow of the Almighty. I will say of the Lord, He is my refuge and my fortress: my God; in Him will I trust. Surely He shall deliver you from the snare of the fowler, and from the perilous pestilence. He shall cover you with His feathers, and under His wings you shall take refuge; His truth shall be your shield and buckler. You shall not be afraid of the terror by night; nor the arrow that flies by day; nor of the pestilence that walks in darkness; nor of the destruction that lays waste at noonday. A thousand shall fall at your side; ten thousand at thy right hand, but it shall not come near you" (Ps 91:1–7).

My *Lord and my God, thank You for being our Keeper and mighty shield of protection. You have proven Your wonderful Truths, time and time again! I love to declare Your glory. Amen!*

Faith In Action

In March 1996, I received divine revelation concerning my mother while I was home worshipping in the spirit. In the vision, I could see my mother's property. I did not visually see my mother, but I saw her home, the landscape, and neighboring homes. At the time, mother lived in a rural community outside of Montgomery, Alabama, known as Ramer.

There was no dialogue, but I knew I needed to pray. Usually I pray in the spirit (tongues) when I'm not sure how to proceed. Not knowing what the issue was, I prayed for my mother health, healing, and protection. I prayed that there would be no problems with her property, and I prayed for her neighbors. I ended my prayer with thanksgiving and gratitude, knowing that the Lord was working in the situation.

The day after the vision and prayer, I received a call from my mother's aunt stating that mother was in critical condition in Baptist

Hospital in Montgomery, and if I wanted to see her alive, I needed to come quickly. The doctors did not expect her to survive.

I immediately called the hospital and identified myself. I asked the nurse if there had been any improvement in my mother's condition overnight. The nurse seemed somewhat hesitant to reveal information over the phone, but I persisted in my quest for information concerning my mother's health. Finally she said, "There was a very slight improvement in your mother's condition but, she is by no means out of danger." I assured her that all I needed to know was that there had been improvement, no matter how slight.

My son and I drove to Montgomery but before we left Miami, I went into intercession and worshipped. I thanked my Heavenly Father for His divine intervention in mother's healing.

When I reached the hospital, mother was in the critical care unit. The lady lying in the room assigned to my mother was unrecognizable to me, but it was my mother. She was critically ill; appearing almost at the point of death. I stayed with her, praying and praising God for her healing. This was my "faith in action!"

When I spoke to the head nurse on duty that day, she stated that mother's condition had drastically improved since her admission, and her recovery was nothing short of miraculous. She further commented, "In my eighteen years as head nurse in this hospital, no one has ever been admitted in your mother's condition and survived. I was so sure that your mother would not survive the night, that when I returned to work the next day, I asked my staff what they had done with her body." The staff told her that mother was in her room. She said, "I had to see for myself." She further declared, "There had to be divine intervention." And it was!

My Heavenly Father had already begun mother's healing process when He prompted me to intercede. Mother was released from the hospital six days after being admitted and made a slow but miraculous recovery.

Children of God, we must understand that our God is Omniscient, all knowing. "For He looks throughout the whole earth and sees everything under the heavens" (Job 28:24). He is Omnipotent, all powerful; "Great is our Lord, and of great power: His understanding is infinite" (Ps. 147:5). He has the power to heal, deliver, and set free. He is Omnipresent, ever-present. The Psalmist said, "Where can I go from Your Spirit? Or where can I flee from Your Presence? If I ascend into heaven, You are there; if I make my bed in hell, behold, You are there. If I take wind of the morning, and dwell in the uttermost parts of the sea, even there, Your hand shall lead me, and Your right shall hold me" (Ps.139:7–10).

God is present everywhere. He is not limited by distance, space, or time. We can never escape from His Spirit. The good news is that those who know and love God are never far from His comforting presence. We are instruments of His grace, mercy, love, and power. He desires to accomplish mighty acts in the earth through His people. My God is incredible!

God prompted me to intercede for my mother and He healed her. He then granted her an additional twelve years of life. As critically ill as my mother was, only God could have performed the miraculous. He did in mother's case. Jehovah-Rapha, the Great Physician (Ex. 15:26; Ex. 23:25) came through, powerfully. How great is our God! How can I fail to praise, honor, trust, serve, and obey Him?

Lord you truly are the Great Physician, thank you for being our merciful Healer!

God Speaks Through His Holy Spirit

God's Spoken Dialogues

In addition to earlier stories I have shared concerning how God has spoken to me on various occasions, I now will share several others. This is not an all encompassing list of times and occasions where God has spoken to me, but these are a few significant events that have been life changing for myself and others. As I stated in a previous chapter, when God speaks to me, sometimes it's a single word, other times it is a phrase, but often, it's a complete dialogue. I am not sure why God chooses to speak to me in this manner; but I never question His approach. I believe He will speak to you as you develop a personal and intimate relationship with Him.

- **<u>September 1, 1996:</u>** God spoke to me and said, "It is done, you're delivered, you've been set free!" During that time, I was dealing with a series of devastating personal, health, family, and emotional issues. I was oppressed, depressed, and spiritually suppressed. There were psychological scars stemming from early childhood traumas that penetrated deep within the crevices of my soul and spirit. Up to that point, my life had been a tapestry woven through with pain. Inter-woven within my life's tapestry, were threads of abuse, abandonment, rejection, and family betrayal. When God spoke His Word of deliverance, my life was forever changed. God has truly set this captive free!

- **November 1996:** God spoke the word, "Windfall." At the time of His spoken Word, I was facing serious financial challenges. My business had nearly slowed to a halt. All my bills were seriously delinquent; bankruptcy appeared to be the only way out. Shortly after His spoken Word, I received an unexpected check in the mail, my sales increased, and God performed one miracle after another to deliver me from total financial destruction. It was during this crisis that I totally learned to live by faith. God proved Himself as Jehovah-Jireh, my powerful Provider. Scripture provides a marvelous account of God's miraculous provision; telling Abraham to offer his long awaited son Isaac as a sacrifice. Trusting God and his faithfulness, Abraham set out to follow the Lord's instructions. At the precise moment, God provided a ram for Abraham's sacrifice, preventing him from harming his son. Abraham named the place Jehovah-Jireh, which means, 'the Lord will provide' (Gen. 22:1–14).

- **February 1997:** During intercessory prayer, God spoke again. He said, "It will never be the same, never be the same. He repeatedly said, "It will never be the same!" And life has not been the same. I have leaned to hear His voice and completely trust Him. Scripture declares, "For I am the Lord: I will speak, and the word that I shall speak shall come to pass; it shall be no more prolonged; for in your days, O rebellious house, will I say the word, and will perform it, says the Lord God" (Ez. 12:25). Surely, the Lord has spoken, and the things which He said, have come to pass.

Heaven Bound

In August 2004, my brother Paul called to inform me that my father had been admitted to University of Alabama Hospital (UAB) in Birmingham, Alabama. The doctors told the family that my father had advanced stage-four colon cancer and a host of other serious medical issues. They did not expect him to recover and the prognosis of him leaving the hospital was slim.

I immediately went into prayer, interceding for my father's recovery. During prayer, the Lord spoke and said, "Nothing will happen before you get there, he's your dad but he's my child; talk to my son about heaven." I asked the Lord to prepare my father's heart to receive a discussion about heaven. I then booked a flight out of Miami and went directly to my father's bedside. I stayed with him night and day for three days, but I had a problem with God's request.

I prayed with my father, we had daily devotion; I read the Bible to him several times a day, and sang his favorite hymns; but I had to figure out how to begin a conversation about heaven. I asked myself the following questions, "Does my father know that he is dying? How will he feel having a discussion about heaven? And how do I begin this discourse?" I knew my father was saved; I had witnessed to him years prior, but I was not sure if he was aware of the doctor's prognosis.

I decided that I would provide my dad with several options and let him choose which topic he wanted to discuss. I selected topics such as love, peace, forgiveness, hope, joy, and heaven. Not surprisingly, when given choices—dad chose *"heaven."* Whew!

I read to my father from the Book of Revelation Chapters Twenty-one and Twenty-Two. We discussed God, Jesus, the Throne of God, the angels, the Book of Life, and the Holy City. He wanted to hear about the pearly gates and the streets of gold. As I read scriptures, my dad closed his eyes and began to smile; as if, visualizing heaven.

About a week after I returned to Miami, my father passed away. My family reported that in his final hours, dad was witnessing about heaven to family, nurses, doctors, and everyone around him. Below you will find a tribute I wrote to summarize my visit with my father.

A Tribute To Dad

One Of The Most Precious Gifts Of God Is A Wonderful Dad
Who Knows And Loves The Lord!
This Is True Of Dad Tower, He Knew And Loved God;
He Presented His Children Before The Lord,
Bowed Down And Worshipped Him.
My Dad Was A Mighty Man Of God!
When He Came To The End Of His Earthly Journey,
Where Sickness Had Weakened His Flesh,
He Placed His Hand In The Master's Hand
And Said, "Father, Give Me Rest!
He Wanted To Talk About Heaven
With Its Twelve Gates Of Pearl, Streets Of Solid Gold,
And The Wonders To Behold!
I Said, "The Walls Are Made Of Jewels And Gems,
Of Every Imaginable Kind!"
No Sickness, Sin, Or Sorrow Can Ever Enter In.
Dad Smiled As We Talked About Heaven
And Said, "I'm On My Way!"
I Said, "If You Get There First, Save A Place For Me."
If I Get There First I Said, "I Will Save A Place For You."
Dad Looked At Me And Smiled.
I Knew What He Was Thinking, He Never Had To Say!
My Dad Thought Of His Family, In His Final Days On Earth.
He Said To Those Around Him, "I Am Heaven Bound,
If You Want To Go To Heaven one day,
You Had Better Learn To Pray!"

God Made Him A Witness, As He Took His Final Breath.
That Is The Reason God Spoke To Me;
"He's Your Dad, But He's My Child,
Talk To My Son About Heaven!"
God Prepared Dad's Heart To Receive His Crown
And His Mansion In The Sky.
I Know I Will See My Dad Again,
When I Take My Perfect Rest,
But For Now, I Will Forever Treasure
The Precious Memories Of My Dad,
As We Reflected On The Wonders Of Heaven
And The Glory That It Holds!
I Will Always Remember The Look In His Eyes,
As I Held His Hand And Rubbed His Face
And Saw His Beautiful Smile!
To Have Had A Dad Like My Dad,
I Am Marvelously And Wonderfully Blessed!

Beyond Expression

On the morning of September 20, 2008, I was home getting dressed to attend the funeral service of my friend's mother. As I was deciding what to wear, the Holy Spirit began a dialogue with me about my mother's funeral. He said, "When the time comes, do not deal with your mother's funeral arrangements in cash, use a check or credit card." I thought it was strange that the Lord would be talking to me about my mother's burial at that moment, but I have learned not to question His wisdom or authority. I thanked God and asked the Holy Spirit to remind me when the time comes. I assumed that in a few years, when the time arrived for me to deal with my mother's death, the Holy Spirit would certainly bring to my memory the things He had spoken in this dialogue, according to (John 14:26).

I was happy and inspired, knowing that my Heavenly Father cares so much for me, and is concerned about every detail of my life. I went about the morning thanking and praising Him for His goodness, grace, mercy, and love.

I finished dressing and my husband and I drove to the church. The funeral was scheduled for 11:00 a.m. After the service, we briefly spoke to our friend and left the church. I decided to go home and take an afternoon nap.

I was resting around 3:30 p.m. when I heard the telephone ring. My husband answered, and I heard him say, "Oh my God, let me get Bettie!" Handing me the telephone; he said, "it's Ethel...something about Momma." I grabbed the telephone and asked my cousin what was wrong? Ethel said, "Bettie, it's Cousin Ida, she's gone!" "What do you mean, gone? Gone where?" I asked my cousin. She said, "I'm so sorry, your mother just passed away!" I screamed into the telephone, "Just passed away! How can this be?"

This was all so shocking! It happened so quickly! One can only imagine the ultimate shock of having such a dialogue and within hours, have the devastating revelation come to pass. I didn't know what to say to Ethel. I needed time to compose myself. I told her that this was such a shock and I would call her later. I thanked her for calling and hung up.

I asked the Lord, why He had not prepared me for my mother's death. He candidly said, "I did." In reality, God did instruct me; I simply did not understand, nor anticipate it occurring, within hours of our dialogue! I thought I would have months, perhaps a year or two, before having to make those arrangements.

I quickly discovered the reason for my Heavenly Father's thoughts concerning the financial dealings of my mother's funeral when her caretaker promptly demanded cash for the burial costs. Armed with foresight, I told her that I did not have cash; the funeral arrangements would be taken care of with a credit card; and I would be handling the details myself.

I was reminded of God's Words, "For my thought are not your thoughts, neither are your ways, my ways" (Isaiah 55:8). God proved this truth— that day!

Our Heavenly Father loves us incredibly. He cares about all things great and small, that pertain to our lives and future. And He always guides, guards, and protects us.

Lord you are our Jehovah-Shammah, the Lord is there (Eze. 48:35). Help us to trust Your Omnipresence, even when we don't understand Your work or Your ways!

Simply Trusting

On Saturday morning December 17, 2011 at approximately 11:30 a.m., I was home cleaning. My husband Charles had not been feeling well for several days. He thought he had the flu and was taking over-the-counter meds to deal with his flu symptoms. That morning, Charles was coughing, wheezing, and trying to get his Asthma under control. He was still lying in bed when the Holy Spirit spoke to me and said, "Go lay hands on him and pray." As the Lord instructed, I went and laid my hands on my husband and prayed for his healing. About forty-five minutes later, Charles said he still did not feel well and was having difficulty breathing. He asked me if I thought he should go to the emergency room. I told him if he felt he needed to go, he should. Charles was trying to resist being admitted so close to Christmas for fear of being hospitalized on Christmas Day.

Unable to maintain at home any longer, my husband asked me to drive him to the emergency room at Jackson Memorial Hospital (JMH) South Campus. He got dressed and we left for the hospital. On the drive, Charles could barely breathe sitting in the car, and asked me to pull the car over so he could get out and stand up. He was able to get more air into his lungs as he stood. We were several blocks from home and about eight minutes from the hospital.

Charles stood outside the car for several minutes and got back inside saying, "I think I can make it!" I began driving those several miles to the hospital, but had to stop again after driving half-a-block. Charles finally said, "Pull-over and call 911." I did, and the paramedics arrived quickly. They rushed my husband into the ambulance and began working on him right away. They told me that, due to his complications, they would be taking him to Baptist Hospital instead of JMH.

They told me to drive ahead but when I reached the hospital, they had not arrived. I thought they would arrive more quickly, since they did not have to stop for traffic signals. I registered and was told to wait; they would notify me when the ambulance arrived.

I waited about seven or eight minutes before the receptionist allowed me to go to my husband's bedside. When I got there, hospital staff and paramedics were rushing around inside. The blinds were closed and I was refused access. They made statements to me like, "things are not looking good; we're working on him; he's going down fast; and there is a fifty-fifty chance of him surviving."

The captain of the paramedic crew finally came out and told me that I should contact my family and if we had any children, I might want to have them there. "Things are not looking good," she said. She told me that after I left the scene, Charles had stopped breathing on his own and they had to stop and intubate (insert a breathing tube) him. That was the reason they had taken so long to reach the hospital. They placed my husband on life-support and he was struggling for survival.

I contacted my daughter and told her to contact our sons and other relatives and get to the hospital as quickly as possible. When I was finally permitted to go to my husband's bedside, he was heavily sedated; in and out of consciousness, struggling for every breath, and fighting for his life. He appeared to be in a great deal of pain and discomfort. Even with the intubation, he appeared to be drowning.

They kept Charles heavily sedated on Propofol to prevent him from trying to extract the breathing tube. I cried out to God, pleading for my husband's recovery. At one point, I stretched my arms across his body, asking the Lord to strengthen him through me. It was such an ordeal observing my husband in a state of semi-consciousness, struggling for his life. But I knew that God was working in the situation.

I could not allow myself to be moved by what I was observing. I needed to trust God; now, more than ever! Why would the Holy

Spirit enjoin me to 'lay hands on him and pray,' if He was not going to heal my husband?

The family arrived quickly and we all stood around watching and praying as my husband continued his struggle for survival. About six hours into the ordeal, we all observed as the Lord suddenly quickened my husband. He opened his eyes and looked around, puzzled to see us all standing there. He gave us a weak thumbs-up and asked, "Where am I?" We told him that he was in the Critical Care Unit at Baptist Hospital. He had no memory of anything after being placed in the ambulance. I knew the strong powerful hand of Jehovah-Rapha had come through once again!

Charles was quickly transitioned from the critical care unit to intensive care, to a recovery room within twelve hours. The medical staff informed us that his left lung had collapsed and that caused an over-exertion of the heart. They stabilized his breathing and inserted a heart defibrillator. I knew the Holy Spirit had granted us the miracle of life, health, and healing once again!

My husband was released from the hospital four days before Christmas. He was able to enjoy Christmas Day with family, watching the grandchildren joyfully open their presents. But His life was the greatest gift to our family that Christmas!

God always gives clear instructions when we are listening. He instructed me to lay hands on my husband and pray. My hands did not heal my husband, but God's power. We are instruments of His grace. Had I continued driving, my husband would not have arrived at the hospital alive. The Holy Spirit working through the medical professionals and me healed my husband that day!

I have learned to trust, rely on, have faith and confidence in, the Omniscient-ever abiding; Omni-potent, all powerful; everlasting; ever-loving; unchanging; never ending; un-relenting, love, and power of Almighty God. He has proven His awesomeness repeatedly in my life and circumstances.

We must allow the Holy Spirit to work through our lives. It is an exciting experience to know that the God of the universe loves us and wants us to partner with Him in service to humanity.

I give all praise, honor and glory to Jehovah-Rapha, my Healer for the blessing of healing and life for my husband!

Chapter Nine

God Speaks Through Supernatural Interventions

Clifford's Final Touch

It has been more than six years since I received that dreadful phone call from the hospital. It was Dr. Willis, my son's health care physician. The words she spoke were devastating, "Mrs. Ferguson this is Dr. Willis, Clifford's heart has stopped and he has no pulse; but don't worry, I won't quit no matter what happens; I will not give up." I heard those words but somehow it did not register that she meant that my son had passed-away and she was performing CPR to try and revive him.

How could it register? For thirty-four years, Clifford had always overcome his Sickle-Cell crisis. Why should this time be different? But there was something vastly different. It seemed as though someone was speaking to me in a dream from some distant place. I needed to wake up, but this was no dream. The voice on the other end of the phone was real. It did not seem urgent, but it was real.

Prior to the call from Dr. Willis, I had received a voice message from Clifford saying, "Hey mom, I need you to pray for me; the doctors can't control my pain—please pray; I love you Mom!" Those were my son's final words to me.

Over the years, Clifford had learned to trust in the power of the prayer of agreement (Matthew 18:19). We would pray and agree for his healing and he would receive treatment and be released quickly from the hospital, in many cases. Sometimes, he would not have to be admitted. For that reason, I was perplexed when Clifford did not call me at work the last time. He knew my work number and he knew my work schedule.

I received his voice message after arriving home from work on the day of his hospital admission. His message was simple; his tone serious. I could detect nervousness in his voice and could tell he was in a great deal of pain.

I rushed to the hospital to be with my son, expecting to chat, as usual, about his ordeal. But I was in for the shock of my life. Upon entering the hospital, I had to wait for what seemed like hours, although it was only about twenty minutes before I was allowed to see Clifford. He was in the Critical Care Unit of Jackson Memorial Hospital in Miami, FL. I signed consent forms, authorizing treatment and waited until I was permitted access to his bedside.

Absolutely nothing could have prepared me for what awaited when I entered his room. Clifford was heavily sedated and struggling for survival. He was hooked up to machines with wires and tubes inserted everywhere. One monstrous machine seemed to be assisting with his breathing. His arms were restrained to prevent him from extracting the tubes. He was struggling to free himself from the restraints with the little strength that remained. For the first time, Clifford appeared scared.

I tried to assure my son that everything was going to be fine. When I spoke, Clifford nodded once to acknowledge that he understood. Knowing I was there calmed him and he ceased struggling. He was unable to speak and never opened his eyes, but remained calm.

Next to his bed, I prayed, quoted healing scriptures, and pleaded with God, but I felt numb, weak, and powerless. I stayed by my son's bed side as long as the hospital staff would permit; which were ten to fifteen minute intervals every two hours. I needed to appear strong for my son, but for the first time—I was devastated and scared too. My mind could not comprehend what God's spirit was communicating.

My eyes focused on the rising and falling of his chest. What is this breathing apparatus? Life-support! What does it mean? How can this be? The seriousness of this situation was debilitating. A part of me knew the seriousness of the situation, but another part reasoned, He'll be fine; he's been through these situations before. But not really! After all, I had never before seen my son this critically ill.

Desperately seeking hope, I literally chased after physicians and other medical staff; anyone who would listen. I bombarded them with a myriad of questions about things I did not understand—simply could not comprehend. "Why is he not responding to me? My son always responds to me. 'Why does his skin feel cool to the touch?' 'Why are his eyes glossed over?' Why...why...why," I pleaded for answers. The doctors gave me the hope and assurance, I desperately needed. "He's young, he's strong, he'll be back to shooting baskets in no time," they responded. Oh, how I wanted to...needed to believe. "Please God let it be true," I cried!

The turmoil in my soul and spirit prevented me from comprehending what my eyes were observing. I talked to God and God talked to me, but I was confused and confounded; everything was muddled, nothing was registering. God was speaking, but I was too numb to comprehend. There was a part of me that knew I was losing Clifford, but another part held on to every thread of hope.

Denial perhaps, but how could I let go? This was my first-born and only biological son. "We have been through so much together. We can overcome this too, we always do," I cried! After all, I am a woman of strong faith and I had prayed in faith, believing the Lord would answer.

During one of our two hour intervals, my family and friends rushed to the church and petitioned God, interceding for Clifford's healing. After about thirty minutes, my husband Charles finally said, "Honey, I believe we have a breakthrough." He felt that the Lord had answered our prayers. Hopeful and grateful for the support, we thanked our friends and left the church. We went home and checked the voice mail before heading back to the hospital and there it was— that voice message from Dr. Willis. I called my daughter, Sonya and we rushed to the hospital.

On the drive to the hospital, something amazing, miraculous, and unexplainable happened. I felt a very firm squeeze on my upper left bicep. This is strange. How can it be? I wondered. Clifford was the only person who had ever touched me in that manner. One of his favorite things to do when recovering from a crisis was to take hold of my left bicep and squeeze; this was a good indicator that he was regaining strength in his hand.

This was the strongest, most firm squeeze of all. The intensity of it almost caused me to wince. There was no mistaking it—this was Clifford's touch! Puzzled, I asked myself, "What does it mean? How is this possible?" Hoping, trusting, and praying that all would be well with Clifford; my husband Charles, daughter Sonya, and I drove in tears and silence.

When we stepped off the elevator on the critical care unit of the hospital, Dr. Willis was standing there. She had escorted another family to the elevator. She recognized me and preceded to tell me that as physicians they do all they can for their patients. She went on to say, "I promised you that I would do all I could for your son, and I did." I listened intently, for the good news, but her next words floored me. "I'm sooo sorry, we lost Clifford," she said.

Devastated, all hope gone, both Sonya and I had to be helped from the floor. Charles gathered us and our belongings. Dr. Willis tried her best to console my family; she led us to a small conference room and answered our questions. Still hoping and searching for answers; and not willing to accept the reality of the situation, I finally asked the doctor what was the possibility of Clifford coming through this ordeal? She assured me that there was no possibility of him pulling through. Emotionally distraught—bereft, I still believed that God could heal Clifford and raise him up. Deep, deep, deep, denial!

When I gathered enough strength, I went to my son's bedside and prayed. I told him that I would always and forever love him. I thanked him for honoring me with *his life and final touch.* I am still in awe of the touch, or how it was possible! I believe it was Clifford's way of saying, "Don't worry mom, all is well. I now am whole, walking on the streets of gold." Although, I cannot explain it, I am forever grateful that God granted me, the miraculous touch; Clifford's final touch!

Today, I am reminded of happier times when Clifford and I had long talks about issues of life and the after-life; wondering what it would be like on the other side. We discussed how we would try to make contact with each other. I never expected it to happen this way!

Call It Intuition

In January 2007, I began taking private piano lessons at the home of a gentleman I had met at a music store in my community. He introduced me to his wife, two of his teenage daughters, and a teenage son. There was another daughter, living on campus, studying at the University of Miami. From all appearances, this appeared to be a happy, loving family.

My instructor taught lessons at the music store but he also maintained a studio in his home, where he taught students of all ages on various instruments. I was happy to be able to schedule lessons around my work schedule and thought I was being taught by one of the best professionals in the business.

A couple of months into my lessons, I was in session when I sensed a strong presence in the room that caused the hairs on my body to stand on edge. I looked around but nothing appeared out of the ordinary. My instructor was sitting on a bench near me at the piano, grading papers. The cat was peacefully napping on top of the piano. Everything appeared normal, but I felt uneasy. I excused myself and left vowing to make up at my next session.

I knew something was not right, but in my zeal to learn to play piano; I quieted the voice of reason and continued. Several lessons later, I again felt a strong presence of some unseen force that sent chills down my spine. I needed to get out of there! I left, again vowing to make up, at my next session. The gentleman had always maintained a high level of cordiality and professionalism with me; and had never been inappropriate. However, I had begun to feel very uneasy and decided that if I continued, it would be at a time when the family would be home and I would not be alone with him. But each time I attempted to make an appointment for my next session, I experienced feelings of intense apprehension and extreme dread.

God was trying to reveal something I could not comprehend. I prayed for my own safety and asked God to bless that family. I knew something was not right but I could not put my finger on it. Call it intuition, if you will. I cancelled my next few lessons, deciding to take time off for spring break.

As I shared my experience with family and friends, they encouraged me to simply quit. "Don't go back!" they warned. I followed their advice and told the instructor that I had a conflict in my work schedule and would not be continuing. He expressed his disappointment and asked me to call when I worked out a new schedule.

About six weeks after I ended my classes, I was home watching the evening news when my piano instructor's face flashed across the television screen. The caption read—"Man murders family and commits suicide." I was devastated to learn that this man had just murdered his wife, the two daughters I had met, and attempted to murder his son, before committing suicide in their home. Fortunately, the son was able to run for safety; taking shelter at the home of a neighbor. This all happened in a nice, quiet neighborhood, in the middle of a weekday afternoon.

I was horrified! I had met this lovely family. I had sat in their home and shared tea, music, and laughter. This was a horrific tragedy that sent shockwaves throughout the entire community. Again, I could only thank my Heavenly Father for keeping me safe from such a horrendous tragedy.

I am truly grateful to the Lord for not allowing me to continue my classes. If not for the grace, mercy, and love of God, I could have been in that home the day the piano instructor decided to murder his family and take his own life. I only wish I had been able to comprehend the message that was being revealed and perhaps, say or do something that could possibly have saved that family. My prayers were simply not enough to save them!

Chapter Ten

God Speaks Through The Church

*C*hristianity and the Christian church began with an outpouring of the promised Holy Spirit and the commencement of the proclamation of the gospel of Jesus Christ. The Book of Acts gives an accurate account of how early Christians responded immediately after Jesus had died on the cross and been resurrected. Acts give realistic portrayals of supernatural revelations that were common occurrences in the early church.

Acts begins with supernatural communication among the resurrected Lord, His apostles, and two angels. Jesus and His eleven apostles were standing on the Mount of Olives. Jesus had just finished telling them to wait in Jerusalem for the baptism of the Holy Spirit. Their initial question shows their lack of understanding of the mission before them. In Acts 1:6 they asked if He would restore the kingdom of Israel at that time.

Jesus had already answered their question in (Matt. 24:36). However, they asked it again anyway. He answered them saying, "It is not for you to know times or seasons which the Father has put in His own power. But ye shall receive power after that the Holy Ghost is come upon you: and you shall be witnesses unto me both in Jerusalem, and in Judea, and in Samaria and unto the uttermost part of the earth" (Acts 1:7–8).

After the promise of power from the Holy Spirit, Jesus was taken up right before their eyes and a cloud received Him (Acts 1:9). While they stood staring in amazement toward heaven, two angels were sent to them saying, "Men of Galilee, why do you stand gazing up into heaven? This same Jesus, who has been taken from you into heaven, will come back in like manner as you saw Him go into heaven" (Acts 1:10–11).

Acts Chapter Two begins with a supernatural explosion. The Holy Spirit arrived on the day of Pentecost, accompanied by extraordinary manifestations of His presence. He filled the Upper Room where they gathered. "And suddenly, there came a sound from heaven as a rushing mighty wind; filling the house where the hundred and twenty were sitting. And there appeared unto them cloven tongues like fire, and it sat on each of them. And they were filled with the Holy Ghost and began to speak with other tongues, as the Spirit gave them utterance" (Act 2:2–4).

The Holy Spirit of God filled the room and empowered the people that day. An international crowd had gathered and heard their own language being spoken, as they witnessed the presence and power of the Holy Spirit on display (Acts 2:11).

The sound of mighty rushing winds and the sight of tongues of fire had attracted a huge crowd to the place where the hundred and twenty believers had just been filled with the Holy Spirit; a supernatural phenomenon was taking place. Some of the people were amazed at what they were witnessing; while others, mocked saying, "These men are drunk" (Acts 2:12–13).

Peter observing both perplexity and confusion stepped forward with the eleven, and boldly lifted his voice to address the crowd (Acts 2:14). Peter's speech was a powerful and dynamic proclamation, inspired by the Holy Spirit. It was the fulfillment of a prophecy spoken in the Old Testament by the Prophet Joel.

Peter proclaimed, "This is what was spoken by the prophet Joel: and it shall come to pass in the last days says God; that I will pour out My Spirit on all flesh; and your sons and your daughters shall prophesy. Your young men shall see visions; your old men shall dream dreams. And on My menservants and on my maidservants, I will pour out My Spirit in those days; and they shall prophesy. I will show wonders in heaven above and signs in the earth beneath; blood and fire and vapor of smoke. And the sun shall be turned into darkness, and the moon into blood, before the coming of the great and awesome day of the Lord. And it shall come to pass that whoever calls on the name of the Lord shall be saved" (Acts 2:16–21).

The coming of the Holy Spirit at Pentecost inaugurated an age of revelation and power. In these days in which we live, it should not be uncommon to witness, our sons and daughters prophesying. Visions and dreams are now normal occurrences for the children of God. There is no age, economic, or gender restriction on the Holy Spirit's power. Because of the Holy Spirit's anointing, we are now empowered to accomplish our God-given assignments. And by faith, any believer can possess the Holy Spirit's power to do the work of Christ. If you read the Book of Acts, you will see the supernatural power of God manifested in every chapter.

Chapter 1. After His death and resurrection, Jesus appeared to the eleven apostles from time to time over a period of forty days and talked with them about the Kingdom of God (v. 3–9). After Jesus ascended into heaven, angels came down and proclaimed to the eleven apostles that Jesus would return in the same manner in which he had ascended— bodily and visible (v. 10–11).

Chapter 2. On the day of Pentecost, a mighty wind and tongues of fire swept through the room where the hundred and twenty were praying, and they all spoke in tongues (v. 2–4). This shows that the anointing of the Holy Spirit is available to all who believe. Christianity is not limited to a select race or group of people. Christ offers salvation to people of all race, cultures, and nationalities (v. 7–8). In verses 16–21, Peter preached an inspirational sermon, quoting the prophetic promise of (Joel 2:28–32).

Chapter 3. The healing of the lame man at the temple gate called Beautiful portrayed power and the glory of Christ (v. 1–13).

Chapter 4. Peter and John's defense of the Gospel message and proclamation of the name and power of the Lord Jesus Christ by whose authority they preached, were examples of preaching inspired by the Holy Spirit (v. 1–12).

Chapter 5. An angel instigated a most profound jail break for the apostles, telling them to go to the temple and give the people the message of life. (v. 19–20).

Chapter 6. Stephen was full of God's grace and power under which he performed miraculous signs and amazing wonders; he spoke so powerfully under the anointing of the Holy Spirit that no one could rebut his wisdom (v. 8, 10).

Chapter 7. As Stephen made his defense before the Jewish high council, being full of the Holy Spirit, he was empowered to look into heaven and see the glory of God and Lord Jesus standing at the right hand of the Father (v. 55).

Chapter 8. Philip went to Samaria preaching the gospel and performing miracles of healing and deliverance (v. 5–7). An angel spoke giving Philip directions for his ministry (v. 26). The Holy Spirit spoke directly to him again in (v. 29). Finally, the Holy Spirit caught Philip up and carried him to Azotus (v. 39–40).

Chapter 9. On his way to bind and persecute Christians, Saul met the Savior on the road to Damascus (v. 3–6). Jesus spoke to Ananias in a vision and sent him to minister to Saul (v. 10–16).

Chapter 10. An angel appeared to Cornelius in a vision and told him to send for Simon Peter (v. 3–8). The Holy Spirit spoke to Peter in a vision and declared that all foods were clean; confirming that what God has cleansed, Peter was not to call unclean (v. 10–16). Peter's vision meant that he should no longer look at the Gentiles as inferior people whom God would not redeem. Again, the Holy Spirit spoke to Peter telling him to accompany the three men Cornelius had sent, doubting nothing (v. 20). Finally, Peter preached to the Gentiles and the Holy Spirit fell on those that heard and they all spoke in tongues (v. 46).

Chapter 11. The prophet Agabus accurately predicted by the anointing of Holy Spirit, that there would be a great famine throughout the land; and it came to pass (v. 28–29).

Chapter 12. An angel of the Lord miraculously freed Peter from jail and certain death (v. 7–11).

Chapter 13. The Holy Spirit spoke to the church at Antioch, telling them to set apart Paul and Barnabas for ministry (v. 2). On his first missionary journey, Paul accurately predicted a judgment of blindness against the sorcerer Elymas—and it came to pass as Paul had said (v. 9–12).

Chapter 14. While preaching at Lystra, Paul commanded a man lame from birth to stand; instantly the man was healed and began to leap and walk (v. 9–10).

Chapter 15. The Holy Spirit communicated to the apostles and elders in the Jerusalem council to lay no unnecessary burdens of the law upon the Gentiles (v. 28).

Chapter 16. On his second missionary journey, the Holy Spirit forbade Paul and his companions to preach the gospel in Asia; or enter Bithynia (v. 6–7). Later on the same journey, Paul received a vision of a man in Macedonia, beckoning them to come and help (v. 9–10). This proved to be the direction in which the Lord was leading Paul's team. God opened the heart of Lydia and she received the gospel preached by Paul (v. 14). Lydia and her household were baptized, and urged Paul's team to be guests in her home (v. 15).

Chapter 17. Paul and Silas went to Thessalonica preaching the gospel to a large group of socially prominent citizens. Some Jew, Greeks and prominent women believed and joined Paul and Silas. (v. 1–4).

Chapter 18. Jesus spoke to Paul in a night vision, telling him, not to be afraid to speak; he would not be harmed; for the Lord had many people in the city of Corinth (v. 9–12).

Chapter 19. Paul laid hand on twelve men in Ephesus who had never heard of the Holy Spirit, and they spoke in tongues and prophesied (v. 1–7).

Chapter 20. Paul spoke supernaturally concerning bonds and tribulations that awaited him in Jerusalem. Paul also gave a prophetic word to the Ephesian elders that they would not see his face again (v. 22–25).

Chapter 21. At Tyre, Paul was urged by disciples speaking under the anointing of the Spirit not to go to Jerusalem (v. 4). Philip had four daughters who were prophetesses (v. 9). Agabus, speaking by the power of the Holy Spirit, prophesied that the Jews of Jerusalem would bind Paul and hand him over to the Gentiles (v. 10–11).

Chapter 22. Paul shared the story of his conversion; how the Lord had appeared to him on the Damascus road (v. 6–16). He also told of his first visit to Jerusalem after his conversion where he had fallen into a trance while praying in the temple; and the Lord warning him to leave Jerusalem, he was being sent to the Gentiles (v. 17–21).

Chapter 23. The Lord appeared to Paul while he was imprisoned in Jerusalem and encouraged him; telling him he would testify of Him in Rome, as he had in Jerusalem (v. 11).

Chapter 24. Paul gave a speech in Caesarea, before Felix, the governor, that was inspired by the Holy Spirit. Paul refuted all his accusers and used every opportunity to witness for Christ (v. 10–26).

Chapter 25. Once again Paul defends himself against false accusers in a speech at Caesarea—this time before Festus, the governor. Paul's speech must be viewed as an inspired utterance by the Holy Spirit in the fulfillment of Jesus' own Words in Luke 12:11–12; 21:10–15 (v. 8–11).

Chapter 26. When King Agrippa came to visit Paul, he recounted the story of his miraculous conversion; how the Lord had appeared to him, transforming his life on the Damascus mission (v. 9–16). Paul took every opportunity to remind his audience that the Gentiles had an equal share in God's inheritance (v. 17–18).

Chapter 27. Paul accurately predicted destruction of the ship meant to take him to Rome (v.10). An angel appeared to Paul during the night, telling him to take courage; there would be no loss of life, but loss of the ship (v. 22–26). Paul warned the crew of pending danger if they abandoned ship; they listened—consequently, their live were spared (v. 30–32).

Chapter 28. In the final chapter, God supernaturally manifested Himself through miracles, signs, and wonders. The first occurred when Paul was bitten on the hand by a poisonous viper and remained unharmed (v. 3–6). Paul later performed a series of miracles in which all the sick on the island of Malta were healed (v. 7–9).

The book of Act presents a clear picture depicting the history of the Christian church and its expansion. Acts shows the awesome miracles and testimonies of heroes and martyrs of the early church—Peter, Stephen, James, Paul, and others. Christian ministry was initiated and held together by the Holy Spirit working in the lives of ordinary people—merchants, travelers, slaves, jailers, church leaders, males, females, Jews, Gentiles, rich, poor, learned, and unlearned. Today, many unsung heroes continue the faith work, empowered by the Holy Spirit—changing the world with the unchanging message that Jesus Christ is Lord of all who call on Him. If you have confessed Jesus as Lord, the Holy Spirit is available to work miracles through your life.

We can allow the Holy Spirit to act as a compass for our lives. He's always pointing us toward what Jesus would say or do. And He wants to make the Father's desires known to us. In any situation, He wants us to know what to do and when to do it. We can trust Him as our guide.

As we have seen, leaders in the early church relied on the Holy Spirit to give them specific and personal guidance—we have the capacity to do likewise. Romans 8:14 and Galatians 5:18 make reference to our being "led by the Spirit," which should be the norm for Christians today. Become an unsung hero for Christ, today!

The Holy Spirit is real. He guides and directs our lives just as He did Christians in the early church. When we are led by the Holy Spirit, we must say yes to the Spirit when He prompts us to take a certain action or say a certain word. We must follow through by doing or saying what He has called us to do or say.

The Holy Spirit often speaks to us in the stillness of our hearts with words of assurance or conviction. When He is directing us away from danger, we often have a heaviness or feeling of trouble, foreboding, or uneasiness in our spirits. When The Holy Spirit is directing us toward helpful things we tend to feel a sense of inner peace and eagerness—a feeling of joy to see what God is about to do.

As did the apostles and heroes of the early church, we must believe for the Holy Spirit's guidance. We are more likely to hear what He has to say to us if we are actively listening for Him to speak. We are much more likely to see the Holy Spirit's direction if we are looking for His signs.

He performed signs, wonders, and miracles in the early church and He is still performing them today in the lives of those that believe.

God Speaks Through Prayer

*P*rayer is one of the avenues through which God speaks to His people. Prayer is the exchange of information between man and his Master. It is one of most common aspects of our communion with God. It is also one of the most important. Prayer brings fellowship, relationship, and discipline to the believer and these will bring the supernatural into our lives.

Prayer is a relationship with the Person of the Holy Spirit. It is a lifestyle. It is an act of worship. It must become second nature, as natural as talking or breathing. Prayer is partnership with the Most High God. This partnership places us in position to hear and receive from our Heavenly Father. When we pray, we are involved in a two-way communion with Ruler of the universe.

Prayer is not a religious ritual that we perform once a day, before a meal, or at bedtime. Prayer is an attitude, it is communion with God. Prayer is not simply a one sided conversation for us to lift up petitions unto God. There must be a sender and a receiver. Either God's Spirit sends and our spirits receive or our spirits send and

God's Spirit receives. There must be an exchange of information between both parties where we speak to the Father and He speaks to us. We must not simply pray, lifting a list of petitions, and expect immediate results. To Hear God speak in prayer, we must pray in faith. We must meditate and patiently wait to hear Him. Hurried prayer will not get the desired results.

Prayer combined with faith, praise, worship, and patience will bring direct communion, where God speaks to us through His Word and His voice. He also speaks through divine inspiration and revelation; through dreams and visions; and many times, through others.

When we pray, we can enter the throne room of heaven. But we must be attentive and undistracted by the cares of this world to hear Him. We must be tuned in to effectively communicate with the Immortal God. Our personal prayer life must be intimate, personal, passionate communion with our Heavenly Father, who is the total source of our lives.

To get desired results when we pray, we must:

1. Pray in faith believing that He hears us (Mark 11:22–24).
2. Pray to the Father in the name of His Son Jesus (John 14:6; 14:13–14).
3. Pray in agreement with His Word; His Word is His will. When we pray according to God's will, He hears and grants the petitions desired (1 John 5:14–15).

We can live in an attitude of prayer constantly being in fellowship with our heavenly Father. He considers it a joy and privilege to fellowship with us and He wants to answer our prayers. Remember, God hears and rewards heartfelt, faith-filled prayers.

When we have the communion of prayer, we will have no problem hearing and recognizing His voice no matter how, when, or where He speaks. Sincere, passionate, heartfelt prayers will open the heart and hands of the Father.

We also must practice hearing God's voice through prayer. We practice hearing God's voice by:

1. Praying: Simply talking to God!
2. Waiting: Patience is the key.
3. Listening: God speaks, be attuned; hear Him!
4. Revelation: His will is revealed.
5. Obedience: Obey His voice; act quickly; follow where He leads!

Fervency In Prayer

The Apostle James said, "The effectual fervent prayer of the righteous availeth much" (Jas. 5:16). This simply means that the adequate, enthusiastic, zealous, intense, passionate prayers of God's righteous, honest, upright, just, and godly men and women have great power and produce awesome results.

To be effective in life and ministry, Christians must develop an effective prayer life. The prerequisites for developing an effective prayer life are: Love of the Father, Son and Holy Spirit; meditation on His Word, praise, gratitude, and thanksgiving.

The Bible tells us that God desires to do great exploits in the earth through the lives of His people (Dan. 11:32). But we will never achieve greatness or do mighty exploits without developing a fervent prayer life. The better we know, hear, and love the Lord, the greater the exploits *He* will accomplish through our lives.

I will now answer several pertinent questions concerning developing communion with God through prayer:

1. How do we build a passionate relationship with God? The relationship of passionate communion with God is simply built on loving God; having an effective prayer life, faith, meditation on God's Word, fasting, praise, and worship.

2. Why do we want fellowship with God? Christians want communion with God because He is our Heavenly Father; the very source of our lives. It gives Him great pleasure to fellowship with us, and because we were created to have fellowship with Him.

3. When should we have fellowship with God? We should seek constant, daily, all day, all night, all time communion and fellowship with God. He is closer than a whisper. He hears every heartbeat!

Prayer is the heartthrob of God! One of the most important benefits we have as Christians is the ability to communicate with God, the Father. We have the ability to show gratitude for His saving, delivering, and protecting power through prayer.

I believe that every major decision that will impact our lives, the lives of others, our businesses, and ministries must be preceded by prayer. It is said that prayer is our key to success and faith unlocks the door. Hallelujah!

There are many types of prayer but I will not address all of them in this Book. This book is designed to lead Christians into a place where we will build an intimate relationship with God, the Father—

through this relationship, begin to hear, discern, and respond to His voice.

Prayers that open the heart and hands of God are:

- Fervent prayers (Jas. 5:16).
- Unceasing; continual prayers (1 Thes. 5:17).
- Prayers of faith (Mark 11:24; Jas. 5:15–16).
- Prayers according to God's Word and His will (1 John 5:15).
- Prayers of praise and adoration (1 Chron. 29:10–13).
- Prayers of thanksgiving and gratitude (Ps. 26:6–7; 28:7; 100:3–5).
- Prayers prayed to the Father in the Name of Jesus (John 14:14; 15:16; 16:23–24).
- Intercessory prayers (Rom. 8:26–28).
- Prayers of agreement (Matt 18:19).

The Holy Spirit revealed to me an interesting revelation from His Word concerning the Prayer of Agreement. Jesus declares in (Matthew 18:19), "That if two shall agree on earth as touching anything that they shall ask, it shall be done for them by My Father which is in heaven." The revelation is that an individual and the Word of God are two. Therefore, when we are in agreement with the Word of God after a revelation has been received from the Holy Spirit, our requests shall surely be granted.

When I receive a revelation from the Holy Spirit, I quickly come into agreement and have received answers from God repeatedly. Often, I have come in agreement with my prayer partners and experienced the fulfillment of God's awesome promises.

Intercessory prayer is also very important. The Apostle Paul prayed and interceded many hours for new believers. For the people of Ephesus, Paul gave continual thanks, making mention of them in his prayers (Eph. 1:16). For the Colossians, Paul prayed and gave thanks to God continually (Col. 1:3).

In Paul's writings to the Corinthians, he instructed the church to pray continually, without ceasing (1 Thes. 5:17). Jesus said, "Men ought always to pray and to not faint" (Luke 18:1).

Ceaseless prayer may seem to be a challenging task for some, but it is the most important benefit we have as Christians. It is the ability to be in constant communication with God the Father and the Lord Jesus Christ.

When we develop the discipline of ceaseless prayer; prayer becomes our first instinct any time we face a challenge, encounter a problem, or run into difficulty. When we maintain an attitude of prayer, we have developed the practice of prayer and it never occurs to us, not to pray.

Simply talk to the Father day and night. Talk to the Father in your home, on your job, in your car. Let Him know what's on your mind. Tell Him when you're hurting, afraid, and lonely. Tell Him when you need, help, hope, and comfort.

If you need answers, talk to Him; facing problems, talk to Him; major life changes and challenges, talk to Him; spirituals decisions, talk to Him. God wants to hear from you, so that you can hear from Him. If you speak to Him, He will speak to you!

Chapter Twelve

God Speaks Through Praise and Worship

Praise is an outward expression of love, adoration, honor, respect, and joy for the Lord. It is the prelude to worship. Praise is where we lift up, extol, exalt, and bestow our love and gratitude on the Father and He draws us deeper into the realm of the Spirit. In this place, we are no longer aware of our surroundings. It may be in the church, synagogue, or home but praise will catapult us into God's presence.

In His presence we will find fullness of joy (Ps. 16:11). Simply praying and worshipping in the spirit almost always takes me into the presence of God. Oftentimes, He speaks— other times I simply bask in the warmth of His peace and presence.

Preludes for worship:

- Wholehearted love (Matt. 22:37–38).
- Humility of Heart (Isa. 57:15; Ps. 8:1, 3–4).
- Holy Reverence (Isa. 6:1–5).

Worship is the individual's expression of heart-felt love, adoration, and reverence for God. It is the highest expression of outpouring love for our Creator. It is gratitude from the depth of our hearts and souls for God the Father and the Lord Jesus Christ.

Man was created to worship God. Our souls long to worship Him. A life without worship is a life void of hope. Without a source for worship, our souls continually search to find joy, peace, hope, love, acceptance, and contentment but come up empty—ever striving. That deep longing inside cannot be filled with money, fortune, fame, or anything outside of the Holy Spirit within us.

We may acquire material things, achieve a level of success, but still find ourselves unfulfilled—we sense that something is missing. The missing link is our spirits' disconnect from God's Spirit, its own life source. Money, wealth, fortune, and fame were never meant to bring lasting satisfaction apart from our relationship with God. Our fulfillment does not lie in things. Our fulfillment is found in the Creator Himself. We were created to worship God and our souls long to worship Him.

Worship automatically flows out of a heart that loves the Lord. Jesus said, "Thou shalt love the Lord your God with all your heart, and with all your soul, and with all your mind. This is the first and great commandment" (Matt 22:37–38). This commandment is a mandate for the dedication of our lives to God above all else. David said, "Delight yourself in the Lord and He shall give you the desires of your heart" (Ps. 37:4). The Father longs to be your heart's deepest desire.

Jesus also said, "Seek first the Kingdom of God and His righteousness and all these things will be added" (Matt. 6:33). All these things include food, clothes, shelter, love, peace, joy, comfort— all the desires of our hearts.

David was called a man after God's own heart (1 Sam. 13:14; Acts 13:22), not because he was righteous. He was called a man after God's own heart because through his numerous trials, tribulations, and temptations; in times of peace and times of war; in times of faith and times of fear, David knew how to worship the Father. His worship pleased God. And in worshipping, he fulfilled the will of God.

David came to know and appreciate the God of his soul. He said, "As the hart panteth after the water brooks, so panteth my soul after thee, O God. My soul thirsteth for God, for the living God" (Ps. 42:1–2).

If we would study the Psalms, we will find David's expressions of worship, adoration, and reverence interwoven throughout all the Psalms of David. David had a deep longing and thirst for the God of his soul. David was also a worshipper and God honored him in peace and in war.

The Apostle John came to understand the awesomeness of God while banished to the Isle of Patmos. John received visions of the Lord in all His glory and majesty, sitting on His heavenly throne (Rev. 4:2–3, 5). John also witnessed all the inhabitants of heaven ceaselessly worshipping God, night and day proclaiming; "Holy, holy, holy; Lord God Almighty, which was, and is, and is to come" (Rev. 4:8–11).

God is holy! He deserves all glory, honor, and praise for His Majesty. He is worthy of ceaseless adoration from all the hosts of heaven and earth, especially His children. Jesus became our sacrificial Lamb and He also deserves our worship (Rev. 5:9, 11–13). Jesus alone stands as King of kings and Lord of lords (Rev. 19:11–16). Let us join King David and Apostle John in offering high praises and worship, in spirit and in truth to our God and King. As we worship, He comes and abides with us and He will speak and reveal His will and amazing promises.

The One We Worship

1. El Shaddai: When Abraham was ninety-nine years old, the Lord appeared to him and said, "I am El-Shaddai —Almighty God" (Gen. 17:1).

2. Elohim: Is plural for God's triune nature and supremacy as Creator. "In the beginning God created the heaven and the earth. So God created man in His own image, in the image of God created He him; male and female created He them" (Gen 1:1; 27). "Now unto the King eternal, immortal, invisible, the only wise God, be honour and glory for ever and ever" (1 Tim. 1:17). God is Creator of all things. Let us worship our Creator.

3. Jehovah Jireh: The Lord will provide. The meaning appears in (Genesis 22:10–14).

4. Jehovah Ropha: The Lord our Healer (Exodus 15:24–26). Let us worship the Lord, our Healer.

5. Jehovah Nissi: The Lord our Banner (Ex. 17:9–15).

6. Jehovah Shammah: The One who is always present (Eze. 48:35).

7. Jehovah Shalom: The Lord our peace (Judges 6:22–24). Our peace rests only in Him.

8. Jehovah Rohi: The Lord is my Shepherd; I shall not want (Ps. 23:1).

To hear Him, we must develop a private time of worship. There we can express our love and bask in God's presence. In His presence, life's cares evaporate into nothingness. In His presence, He showers us with His love, peace, joy, and honors us with the pleasure of hearing and knowing what is in His heart.

When I enter into that place of worship, the Father shows me incomprehensible things; hidden things; future things. It is as if He takes my hand and says, "Come, let Me show you My plans, let Me show you your future!" Let us worship with a purpose—the purpose of loving God and hearing His voice.

God Says Yes!

On February 22, 2009 God spoke to me during high praise and worship, delivering the following message for Faith In Action Ministries.

The very next day, I received one of the greatest miracles of my life. I believe this is also a word for the body of Christ. Receive it and be blessed!

God is saying yes...

God said, it's already done, trust Me

Let Me be God and you be My child.

You have been asking for increase in health, wealth, and healing.

You have been asking for increase in spirituality.

God says, YES!

He is giving increase in hope & strength (emphasis mine).

Increase is here. People need to know that I am God almighty.

I have all power in my hands, says God.

The wait is over...come up in me; I will make your joy full.

I only ask for your faithfulness and obedience.

You don't have to act a certain way, you are already mine.

No one can snatch you out of my hands...you are mine.

I love you with an everlasting love. FOREVER!

Trust me for you healing...trust me like never before and try me.

I will never fail you. There is no failure in me, only victory!

Be my child and watch me take care of you and all your needs.

You are mine...I have an unquenchable thirst for you.

Let me show you how I can and will do exceedingly,
abundantly more than you can ask or think.
TRY Me and KNOW Me!
I am God…I have all power in my hands.
Prove Me and see if I will not rebuke the devour for your sake.
I thirst for your attention…I thirst for your love.
Draw nigh unto Me and I will draw nigh unto you
and show you My mighty power!
Trust Me and lean not to your own understanding;
Acknowledge Me and I will direct your path.
I want to give you the desires of your heart.
I AM GOD!

Hearing God Through Faith

According to the King James Version of the Bible, "Faith is the substance of things hoped for, the evidence of things not seen" (Hebrews 11:1). Another way of stating it is: "Faith is confidence that what we hope for, will actually come to pass." It is affirming the unbelievable with confident conviction. Our confidence says, "Although I don't see it yet, I have assurance it will materialize." Faith links confidence, assurance, anticipation, and materialization.

What we believe today should govern our actions tomorrow and in the future. Faith is believing in God's character. It is believing that God is who He says and will do what He promises. The true demonstration of faith and confidence in God says, "I believe God's promises, even though I don't see them materializing yet." Faith is confidence that what God promised, He will accomplish.

We can replenish our hearts with faith by deeply pondering on the Holy Scriptures and remembering that God's Word is the absolute truth and we can totally rely upon it. God literally cannot lie. Scripture says, "God is not a man, that He should lie, neither the son of man, that He should repent" (Numbers 23:19).

What God has said, He will accomplish, and what He has spoken shall come to pass. Jesus provided an eternal fact in the words of (Matthew 7:7), "Ask, and it shall be given you; seek, and ye shall find; knock, and it shall be opened unto you."

In order to get the full benefits that faith in God offers, we must believe and treasure His Word. We must reverence it and have a willingness of heart to hear and obey. This is the disposition of faith and believing. Having a disposition of faith and believing is a willingness to believe God in spite of all contradictions. Such a sentiment is pleasing to God, and will bring His blessings into our lives.

We must remember: our faith is in the God who framed the entire universe by His spoken Words. By this, we understand that His Words have tremendous and extraordinary power. Faith is an attitude and an action. It is a lifestyle. Habbakuk 2:4 affirms, "the just shall live by faith." Hebrews 11:6 declares, "Without faith it is impossible to please God: for he that cometh to God must believe that He is, and that He is a rewarder of them that diligently seek Him." This is a promise that God actually rewards our faithfulness.

According to Romans 12:3, every believer has been given at least, a measure of faith. Faith was the prerequisite to receiving salvation. And every born again believer has heard God's voice. A believer is one who has heard the Gospel of Jesus Christ—believed, been saved; thus, is now born again. It was God's voice that called us to Him; it was His precious Holy Spirit that drew us with strings of love to receive His awesome salvation message.

Jesus said, "No one can come to Me unless the Father who sent Me draws him" (John 6:44). Therefore, we were conceived into God's family by faith, and we received that faith from our heavenly Father through the voice of His precious Holy Spirit.

Now let us consider how faith works and how to receive it. Faith is acquired by hearing and applying God's Word. Scripture teaches that, "Faith comes by hearing and hearing the Word of God" (Rom. 10:17). Therefore, the more of God's Word we hear, the more faith we will develop. And with more faith, we can believe God for more of His promises.

Hearing God's Word is vital, it is how we receive and increase our faith. If we are to overcome the trials and temptations that will come as a result of our Christian walk, we must possess strong, unwavering faith.

Obstacles To Hearing God

There are many keys to hearing the voice of God. I have outlined some of them in this book. We must follow certain steps to grow closer and align ourselves with God's will to systematically hear Him. Intimate communion, praise, worship, prayer, faith, and the Bible are all important avenues that may lead us to our destination of hearing God speak. But no matter how much we desire to have communion with God, there will always be obstacles.

We will find ourselves constantly battling other agendas. Our own agendas, family agendas, jobs, friends, worldly influences, and temptations that Satan use to entice us, all must be resisted in order to remain close enough to hear the still small voice of God. We must align our priorities to His will.

If we allow other influences to take priority in our lives, we will be less inclined to hear Him, or we may become totally desensitized to His voice.

In the midst of all the chaos in our lives today, we must take time to reflect on God's grace, mercy, love, and goodness. We must set aside time to shut out the world and privately commune with our God, in silence. Remember, it was in a "still small voice" that God spoke to Elijah (1Kings 19:12). I have heard the still small voice of God on many occasions, and you too can expect God to speak to you in your quiet times of communion with Him.

If we are not careful, however, we will find ourselves being drawn by the pull of busyness, and worldly influences. It is then, that we become less sensitive to the voice of our Lord. His will is no longer a priority as we become preoccupied with other things. Let us not become proud, selfish, and covetous. Let us not become more concerned about what others think than spending time with the Lord.

If we allow money, the accumulation of wealth, and worldly possessions to become a priority, we will quickly lose our godly perspective.

Early in my walk with the Lord, I was at a point where I was really struggling financially. I had made a series of bad financial decisions and poor choices. I felt desperate and prayed for God to bless me with a financial miracle. I thought my heart and spiritual priorities were in order. But I was totally surprised when in response to my prayer, God simply said, "James 4:3."

I had not acquired enough Bible knowledge to know what it meant, so after my prayer—I opened the Bible to (James 4:3) and read the following words, "ye ask and receive not because ye ask amiss that ye may consume it upon your lusts.

I was totally astounded by God's response. Didn't He know how serious this was? Didn't He see my dilemma? Didn't God see my desperation? I learned that God looks at our hearts. He is not moved by crisis, dilemmas, or desperation—faith moves God.

The most important lesson I learned was that the Father promises to meet our need, not our lusts. Scripture says, "But my God shall supply all your *needs* according to His riches in glory by Christ Jesus" (Phil. 4:19). Although my needs were real to me, God saw my greatest needs. I first needed to learn the biblical principles of finance and money management.

Fear

Fear is lack of faith. It is a strong and powerful deterrent to faith in our Creator. Fear causes anxieties that will separate us from the voice and presence of God. It limits our capacity to fully trust God. And if we don't trust Him, we cannot please. "For without faith it is impossible to please Him" (Hebrews 11:6).

God tells us, "Don't be afraid, for I am with you. Do not be discouraged, for I am your God. I will strengthen you and help you. I will hold you up with my victorious right hand" (Isa. 41:10 NLT). This is an amazing promise from the Father. It helps us understand God's faithfulness.

We can remain fearless because: (1) God is with us, "For I am with you." (2) God has established a relationship with us, "I am your God." And God provides assurance of his help, strength, and victory. (3) "I will strengthen, help, and hold you up." We have the ability to claim our position as a child of God and overcome fear by applying His Word to our lives.

I personally have forfeited numerous blessings by walking in fear, not fully understanding the power of God. And I believe that we, the children of God, have been denied blessings of monumental proportion because of fear. Like Peter, we considered the boisterous conditions—took our eyes of Jesus and began to sink (Matt. 14:25–31).

Each of us will face fear at some point; it is what we do with it that matters most. The disciples lived and walked with Jesus, they watched Him perform countless miracles, yet at times, they doubted Him.

Thank God for David—in the midst of death and despair; he said, "Yea, thou I walk through the valley of the shadow of death, I will fear no evil; for thou art with me; thy rod and thy staff they comfort me. Thou prepareth the table before me in the presence of mine enemies: thou anointest my head with oil; my cup runneth over. Surely goodness and mercy shall follow me all the days of my life: and I will dwell in the house of the Lord forever" (Ps.23:4–6).

Pride

Pride is a huge obstacle to hearing from God. It completely obstructs our relationship with our heavenly Father. Lucifer gives us an example of what happens when we succumb to pride.

Lucifer led worship in heaven. He walked close to the throne of God until he became prideful and wanted to usurp God's authority. Pride caused him to rebel against God and contributed to his ultimate fall from God's grace.

Isaiah 14:12–14 tells us how it happened, "How art thou fallen from heaven, O Lucifer, son of the morning! How art thou cut down to the ground, which didst weaken the nations! For thou hast said in thine heart, I will ascend into heaven, I will exalt my throne above the stars of God: I will sit also upon the mount of the congregation, in the sides of the north: I will ascend above the heights of the clouds; I will be like the most High.

Ezekiel 28:12–19 tells us that God created Satan as a beautiful angel. But he lusted after God's position and rebelled against the Creator because of his beauty and was consequently cast to earth along with his coconspirators. He forgot that his wisdom, beauty, and splendor were gifts from God. Nothing on earth will cause us to fall faster or further from God's grace than the sin of pride.

Here are a few examples of how God really feels about pride:
  (1) God hates pride (Pro. 6:17).
  (2) Pride goes before destruction, and a haughty spirit before a fall (Pro. 16:18).
  (3) Haughty eyes, a proud heart, and evil actions are all sin (Pro. 21:4 NLT).
  (4) He who is of a proud heart stirs up strife, but he who trusts in the Lord will be prospered (Pro. 28:25).

Impatience

We must learn to wait for God's timing. Failure to wait on God and getting ahead of Him greatly obstructs and hinders our relationship with Him. It limits God's ability to accomplish His will in our lives. David admonishes us to rest in the Lord and wait patiently on Him (Ps. 37:7). The psalmist said, "Be still and know that I am God" (Ps. 46:10).

Waiting is a fact of life when it comes to our hearing from God. When we pray and seek God, He can—but does not always answer us instantaneously. Sometimes He says, yes; sometimes He says no; and sometimes He says wait. Often God makes us wait for the answer, but He always answers in His timing. When we wait on Him, it shows that we trust Him.

Waiting for God's help requires lots of patience. It is not always easy but has great benefits. David said, "I waited patiently for the Lord to help me, and He turned to me and heard my cry. He lifted me out of the pit of despair, out of the mud and mire. He set my feet on solid ground and steadied me as I walked along. He has given me a new song to sing, a hymn of praise to our God. Many will see what He has done and be amazed; they will put their trust in the Lord" (Ps. 40:1–3 NLT).

Look at the blessings David received by waiting on God: (1) God lifted him out of despair. (2) Gods set his feet on solid ground. (3) God steadied him as he walked; and (4) God put a new song of praise in his mouth.

If we want to hear God speak, we must learn to wait— patience is key. After you have prayed, sit still in silence and meditation. In the beginning, patience was one of the most difficult aspects of God's grace for me to learn. I have discovered that blessings may be delayed until we have gone through the trial of waiting. While we wait, we can simply express adoration for our Lord and Savior.

Impatience can lead to the sins of self-will and rebellion. It caused God to reject King Saul. God had anointed Samuel as priest for Israel. It was his duty to lead worship and sacrifice the burnt offerings before God. When Samuel did not come in the appropriate time, Saul looked at the conditions and took matters into his own hands. He sacrificed the burnt offerings himself; thus, disobeying God (1 Sam. 13:8–9).

Saul got ahead of God appointed man and caused his own downfall. Samuel said to Saul, *"You have done foolishly. You have not kept the commandment of God. The Lord would have established your kingdom over Israel forever, but now your kingdom shall not continue"* (1 Sam. 13:13–14). Saul made plenty of excuses for his disobedience but Samuel saw the real issue—rebellion and impatience. Impatience will cause forfeiture of God's blessings.

It seems as though God delights in rescuing His people at the last moment. We must wait on the Lord, even when it seems as though He may not respond in time. One of my father's favorite statements was, "He might not come when you want Him but He's always on time." Remember: it's His timing, not ours.

Unforgiveness

Unforgiveness is a serious deterrent to communion with God. It seriously hampers our ability to fellowship with Him or hear Him. Jesus commands us to forgive. He said, "And when ye stand praying, forgive, if ye have ought against any: that your Father also which is in heaven may forgive your trespasses, but if ye do not forgive, neither will your Father which is in heaven forgive your trespasses" (Mark 11:25–26). He also said if we refuse to forgive others, The Father will refuse to forgive us (Matt. 6:14–15). When we refuse to forgive others, we are denying our common ground as sinners in need of forgiveness.

If unforgiveness remains unchecked, it will cause bitterness to habitate in the depth of our souls and spirits. There it can grow and become very destructive. At the heart of unforgiveness is a root of bitterness. It is the mainspring of many physical, emotional, psychological, and spiritual problems in the world today, even among Christians.

We will all have to deal with unforgiveness, at some point. The Apostle Paul tells us how when he said, "Let *all* bitterness, wrath, clamor, and evil speaking, be put away from you, with all malice, and be kind to one another; tenderhearted, forgiving one another, even as God in Christ forgave you" (Eph. 4:31–32). When Paul spoke of bitterness, wrath, clamor, and evil speaking, he was describing the monstrosity and ugliness of the "spirit of unforgiveness."

The "spirit of unforgiveness" goes far beyond a temporary unwillingness to forgive. It develops when one chooses to remain indefinitely in the unforgiveness mode. Forgiveness frees us from the slavery of sin. It brings joy equally to both the benefactor and recipient of forgiveness.

I have heard people with the spirit of unforgiveness say, I will forgive, but I won't forget. That's an excuse that keeps them from experiencing the true freedom that forgiveness brings. It inhibits our worship, preventing communion with our Father.

Unforgiveness is a choice. It is a devastatingly bad choice—for relationships, for the cause of Christ, and for the one who refuses to free themselves from the bondage of unforgiveness.

We all have been hurt, are now hurting, will be hurt, or have the propensity to hurt someone. Pain is inevitable and unavoidable. Please understand, "no pain is so deep and widespread that it goes beyond the power of God's forgiveness.

Unforgiveness is a sin that leads to bitterness which ultimately leads to separation from God. Jesus said, "Forgive and you will be forgiven" (Luke 6:37). "For if you forgive men their trespasses, your heavenly Father will also forgive you: But if you forgive not men their trespasses, neither will your Father forgive your trespasses" (Matt. 6:14–15).

Forgiveness might be difficult, but unforgiveness is disobedience to God, which can lead to our demise. When we free others from indebtedness, we are in essence, able to see them as Christ sees them—blessed and forgiven. Anger, bitterness, and unforgiveness no longer have the power to rule our decisions, freeing us to have loving communion with our heavenly Father. If we desire to hear the voice of God, we must forgive.

Worldliness

When we were born again, we became like foreigners to this earthly domain, en route to our heavenly home. This world with its attraction of grandeur should no longer hold our attention. We must beware however, because the world's grandiosity can strongly appeal to our fleshly appetites.

The Bible forbids love of the world. Apostle John said, "Do not love the world or the things in the world. If anyone loves the world, the love of the Father is not in him; for all that is in the world—the lust of the flesh, the lust of the eyes, and the pride of life—is not of the Father but is of the world" (1 John 2:15–16).

Worldliness is not limited to external behavior—the people we associate with, the places we go, the activities we enjoy. Worldliness is also internal because it begins in the heart and is characterized by three attitudes, according to John: (1) Lust of the flesh; craving for physical pleasures and preoccupation with gratifying those pleasures. (2) Lust of the eyes; craving for things—coveting and accumulating things and bowing to materialism. (3) The pride of life; pride in our achievements and possessions—obsession with one's status.

When the serpent tempted Eve in the Garden of Eden (Gen. 3:6), it was in these three areas. When Satan tried to tempt Jesus in the wilderness, these also were his areas of attack (Matt. 4:1-11).

Jesus responded to each of those temptations by appealing to the unchanging Word of God. "It is written!" We can successfully overcome the tempter and his temptations by knowing and quoting the Word of God…"It is written," accompanied by the appropriate Scripture!

The Father is not only concerned about our behavior, He's has great concern for our relationships. Once I formed a business and brought in a partner to assist with marketing and product distribution. The business quickly began taking a downward spiral when I discovered my partner's deceptive practices.

I cried out to God in despair and received this rebuke, "What business have you being in business with an unbeliever?" I quickly dissolved the partnership and launched out solo.

Paul warns, "Be ye not unequally yoked together with unbelievers: for what fellowship hath righteousness with unrighteousness? And what communion hath light with darkness?" (2 Cor. 6:14).

We sometimes quote this scripture in reference to choosing a marriage partner but while it is certainly an appropriate application—marriage is not the only concern, we should apply this Scripture to all of life's relationships and partnerships.

Although attractively camouflaged, Satan uses traps, temptations, and the allure of worldly pleasures to separate us from God. If we avoid these dangers, we will enjoy intimate fellowship and sweet communion with our heavenly Father. And He will speak to us!

Chapter Fifteen

God's Call

*G*od speaks to His people but what is He saying today? He is calling His people to salvation. He is calling us to sanctification, purity, and holiness. He is calling us to sacrifice, witness, and service.

God's Call to Salvation

The Father is sending forth the call to those for whom His Son died. He is saying, "That if you shall confess with your mouth the Lord Jesus, and shall believe in your heart that God hath raised Him from the dead, you shall be saved. For with the heart man believeth unto righteousness; and with the mouth confession is made unto salvation" (Rom. 10: 9–10).

He is saying, "Come unto me, all ye that labor and are heavy laden, and I will give you rest" (Matthew 11:28). He is knocking on our heart's door and asking to come in."Behold, I stand at the door, and knock: If any man hears my voice, and open the door, I will come in to him and will sup with him and he with Me" (Revelation 3:20).

This statement was made to the Laodicean Church. It was rich but complacent. They were self-satisfied but did not have the presence of Christ among them. Christ knocked at the door of their hearts, but they were busy enjoying worldly pleasures and didn't know He was trying to enter.

The pleasures of this world; money, security, and material possessions may bring temporary satisfaction but it can make us indifferent to God, the church, and the Bible. If we leave the door of our heart constantly open to God, we will have no trouble hearing his knock or heeding His voice. Letting Him in, is our only hope for lasting joy and fulfillment.

God's Call To Sanctification

The Father's ultimate will is that we be conformed to the image of Christ. "For whom He did foreknow, He also did predestinate to be conformed to the image of His Son, that He might be the firstborn among many brethren" (Romans 8:29). The process of being conformed to the image of Christ will not be complete until we come face to face with Him, but knowing that it is our ultimate destiny should motivate us to purify ourselves. To purify ourselves means that we must keep ourselves morally pure; free from the corruption of sin. God purifies us (1 John 3:3) but it is our responsibility to remain morally fit.

We are confirmed in the image of Christ by reading and heeding His Word; by studying His life through the Gospels, by spending time in prayer, by being filled with His Spirit, and by doing His work. When these are accomplished in our lives, we will have no trouble hearing His voice and following where He leads.

God's Call To Purity And Holiness

God provides the power and the path for these to be accomplished in our lives. God's call to us in (Lev. 20:7) is, "Sanctify yourselves therefore and be ye holy: for I am the Lord your God." He calls His children to walk in His ways. He calls us to sanctification and holy living. "According as His divine power hath given unto us all things that pertain unto life and godliness, through the knowledge of Him that hath called us to glory and virtue" (2 Peter 1:3).

We become more like Christ as we learn to abide in Him according to His Word. God Himself empowers us to lead a godly life, because we don't have the natural resources to be truly godly, but by grace He allows us to share in His divine nature in order to keep us from sin.

God's Call To Sacrifice

God calls all who follow Him to be willing to give of their best for Christ. This always demands sacrifice. It may be sacrifice of your time, talent, or resources—any or all of them. The sacrifice may even call for persecution. "Yea, and all that will live godly in Christ Jesus shall suffer persecution" (2 Tim 3:12). Persecution is inevitable for all who desire to live in a godly manner. Paul's charge to Timothy was that those who are willing to live for Christ will suffer persecution. Therefore, do not be surprised when you are misunderstood, persecuted, criticized, or falsely accused. People may even try to harm you because of your beliefs or the way you live. Do not fear because God has given us the finest example in the sacrifice of His Son.

Jesus was in all points tempted like we are, yet He was without sin (Heb. 4:15). It is comforting to know that Jesus faced a myriad of temptations, trials, and tests but remained sinless. He shows that we do not have to give in when facing the lure of temptation. "For He hath made Him to be sin for us, who knew no sin; that we might be made the righteousness of God in Him" (2 Cor. 5:21). Scripture further declares, "Therefore, in all things He had to be made like His brethren, that He might be a merciful and faithful High Priest in things pertaining to God, to make propitiation for the sins of the people (Heb. 2:17–18). Also see (1Pet. 2:22–24; Is. 53:3–6).

God's Call To Witness

Jesus said, "But ye shall receive power, after that the Holy Ghost is come upon you: and ye shall be witnesses unto me both in Jerusalem, and in all Judaea, and in Samaria and unto the uttermost part of the earth" (Acts 1:8).

The Great Commission was given to the local church but we are the local church! Every Christian has been called by God to be a witness for Christ. The voice of God is not silent. He speaks to the heart of His people and calls them to follow. God wants our willingness to go where that He leads. And He will order our steps. To the uttermost parts of the world, our mission is to live and spread the gospel of Jesus Christ.

God loves us so much that He sent His Son, Jesus to take our place and to die for us. He did this so that we could once again have fellowship with Him. In the book of Hebrews we see that we can have access to God's very presence, "Having boldness to enter the Holiest by the blood of Jesus, by a new and living way" (Hebrews 10:19–20).

God wants us, blessed and successful in the plan has established for our lives, so that we can be a reflection of His love and blessings in the Earth. In (Jeremiah 29:11–13), the Lord makes clear His intentions for you and me, "For I know the thoughts that I think toward you, saith the Lord, thoughts of peace and not of evil, to give you an expected end. Then shall ye call upon me, and ye shall go and pray unto me, and I will hearken unto you. And ye shall seek me, and find me, when ye shall search for me with all your heart."

It is God's desire to walk with and communicate with His children. He wants to talk to us. And He wants us to listen and talk to Him. Let the Father lead you by His voice today! It is a glorious experience.

God's Call To Service

God has equipped us and called us to serve others in the name of the Lord Jesus. There is no Christian that God has not called to serve (1 Corinthians 12:18). He has strategically placed each of us exactly where He wants us in the body. There is no Christian to whom God has not given the spiritual gifts and abilities needed to accomplish His will for their lives.

His call may be general or specific. The key is to surrender our wills to His will and allow Him to accomplish great things through our lives. Now let us examine our call to service. Where is God calling you to serve? What is He saying? Where is He leading? Seek Him and He will show you the way to Truth and Light! Read First Corinthians Chapter 12 and discover where God wants you to join Him in service to the body of Christ today!

Conclusion

*D*o you feel that God wants to speak to you? Then listen up! Open up your heart! God might be trying to get through all the clutter in your life. Open up your heart and hear Him. He speaks to those who are willing to hear.

You can hear the voice of God. In these pages I have reiterated repeatedly the fact that God will speak to you. What does it take to systematically hear God's voice? It takes relationship. This relationship comes from being in close communion with Him. It is a friendship where you begin to know God; knowing Him requires spending time with Him. It requires friendship and fellowship. Patience is also important if you are beginning a journey of hearing God speak.

To hear God speak, you must be prepared. God is not on a time schedule. He is always available to speak. He may speak in a quiet private time and place. He may speak in a crowded arena but when He speaks, you will know and hear Him if you have cultivated the relationship and become familiar with His voice. God can speak through clutter; however, we can hear Him most clearly in quietness. Quiet your soul; meditate on His Word, extol and reverence Him; then patiently wait. I encourage you to learn the art of listening for His voice.

Jesus said, "My sheep hear my voice, and I know them, and they follow Me" (John 10:27). When you develop that relationship, you will recognize His voice. Think of your current relationships, you can distinguish between the voices of your spouse, each of your children, and you can distinctly recognize the voice of all your friends. Become a friend of God and you will hear Him. The mystery of God will dissolve when you know how deeply He loves and wants to be your constant companion. Let God speak to you today...your life will never be the same!

Begin now. Find a quiet place, open your bible, and begin to talk to God. Read His Word out loud, it will build your faith. The Bible says, "Faith comes by *"hearing"* the word of God (Rom. 10:17). Pray and ask God to reveal His voice.

If you have not done so, make Jesus Christ your Lord and Savior. Pray this simple prayer with me. "Jesus, I come to you now. I repent of all my sins and ask You to forgive and cleanse me by Your blood. I now make you Lord of my life. Fill me with the Holy Spirit and do a work in me that will produce noticeable results. Transform me by Your power and love. Teach me to live victoriously in You.

Reveal your voice to me and help me to fully understand that I have been accepted into the family of God. I pray in faith, expecting everlasting results, in Jesus' name. Amen!"

If you prayed this prayer or if you have had the experience of hearing God speak, I want to hear from you. Let me know how hearing His voice has transformed your life.

Please contact me at: bettieferguson@bellsouth.net.

Write to: P.O. Box 971002

       Miami, FL 33197-1002

CPSIA information can be obtained at www.ICGtesting.com
Printed in the USA
LVOW040613300113

317763LV00003B/10/P